BRONX EPITAPH

OTHER BOOKS BY STEVEN K. WAGNER

Perfect: The Rise and Fall of John Paciorek, Baseball's Greatest One-Game Wonder (2015)

Seinsoth: The Rough-and-Tumble Life of a Dodger (2016)

The Four Home Runs Club: Sluggers Who Achieved Baseball's Rarest Feat (2018)

Game Won: How the Greatest Home Run Ever Hit Sparked the 1988 Dodgers to Game One Victory and an Improbable World Series Title (2021)

BRONX EPITAPH

*How Lou Gehrig's "Luckiest Man" Speech
Defined the Yankee Legend*

STEVEN K. WAGNER

EXCELSIOR
EDITIONS

Cover image: Lou Gehrig wipes away tears during his "Luckiest Man" speech. Murray Becker. © The Associated Press.

Published by State University of New York Press, Albany

© 2023 State University of New York

All rights reserved

Printed in the United States of America

No part of this book may be used or reproduced in any manner whatsoever without written permission. No part of this book may be stored in a retrieval system or transmitted in any form or by any means including electronic, electrostatic, magnetic tape, mechanical, photocopying, recording, or otherwise without the prior permission in writing of the publisher.

Excelsior Editions is an imprint of State University of New York Press.

For information, contact State University of New York Press, Albany, NY. www.sunypress.edu

Library of Congress Cataloging-in-Publication Data

Name: Wagner, Steven K., author.
Title: Bronx epitaph : how Lou Gehrig's "Luckiest Man" speech defined the Yankee legend / Steven K. Wagner.
Description: Albany : State University of New York Press, 2023. | Includes bibliographical references and index.
Identifiers: LCCN 2022022892 | ISBN 9781438491806 (pbk : alk. paper) | ISBN 9781438491790 (ebook)
Subjects: LCSH: Gehrig, Lou, 1903–1941 Luckiest Man. | Gehrig, Lou, 1903–1941—Oratory. | Gehrig, Lou, 1903–1941—Philosophy. | Speeches, addresses, etc., American. | Baseball players—United States—Quotations. | New York Yankees (Baseball team)—History—20th century.
Classification: LCC GV865.G4 W34 2023 | DDC 796.357092 [B]—dc23
LC record available at https://lccn.loc.gov/2022022892

10 9 8 7 6 5 4 3 2 1

For Dad, whose love for sports lives on in his children. And, for Mom.

For Rob, Scott, and Kristi.

CONTENTS

List of Illustrations — ix

Preface — xiii

Acknowledgments — xix

Introduction — 1

Chapter 1 Fans — 13

Chapter 2 A Bad Break — 25

Chapter 3 Luckiest Man — 33

Chapter 4 Men in Uniform — 41

Chapter 5 An Honor — 47

Chapter 6 Empire Builder — 57

Chapter 7 Grand Little Fellow — 65

Chapter 8 The Greatest Manager — 75

Chapter 9 My Roommate — 83

Chapter 10 Across the River — 91

Chapter 11	The Yankees Family	101
Chapter 12	Mother-in-Law	113
Chapter 13	Mom and Pop	119
Chapter 14	Tower of Strength	129
Chapter 15	Awful Lot to Live For	137
Epilogue		147
Afterword		157
Appendix		163
Notes		169
Selected Bibliography		181
Index		183
About the Author		193

ILLUSTRATIONS

Figure I.1	Lou Gehrig at Columbia University, ca. 1923.	3
Figure 1.1	Babe Ruth signs his autograph for fans at Griffith Stadium in Washington, DC, in 1937, two years after retiring.	15
Figure. 1.2	Brooklyn Dodgers fans voice their enthusiasm during the 1916 World Series.	18
Figure 1.3	Among the fans in attendance for Yankee Stadium's first game was President Warren G. Harding (*right*), seated with dignitaries (April 24, 1923).	20
Figure 1.4	Fans line up at the Yankee Stadium ticket booth in 1923 to, as Lou Gehrig intimated in his farewell speech, express their kindness and encouragement.	23
Figure 2.1	Joe McCarthy (*left*) joins Washington Nationals manager Bucky Harris to open the 1939 baseball season by raising a flag over the Nationals' home field.	28
Figure 3.1	Lou Gehrig in 1924, the year before he joined the Yankees. *New York Daily News*.	34
Figure 3.2	Paul Krichell, the Yankees scout who discovered Lou Gehrig, in 1911.	37
Figure 4.1	Bob Meusel (*right*), a member of the Yankees' feared Murderers' Row, chats with brother Emil "Irish" Meusel of the New York Giants, 1923.	43

Figure 4.2	Bob Shawkey warms up with the Philadelphia Athletics in 1914, one year before joining the Yankees. He retired after the team's legendary 1927 season.	45
Figure 5.1	Jacob Ruppert at Yankee Stadium.	48
Figure 5.2	Andy Coakley, Gehrig's coach at Columbia University, ca. 1910.	50
Figure 5.3	Jacob Ruppert (*right*) with baseball commissioner Kenesaw Mountain Landis and an unidentified boy.	52
Figure 6.1	Ed Barrow, 1903.	58
Figure 7.1	Miller Huggins.	66
Figure 7.2	Miller Huggins greets Washington Senators player-manager Clyde Milan prior to a 1922 game.	69
Figure 8.1	American League manager Joe McCarthy (*left*) shakes hands with National League manager Bill Terry before the 1937 All-Star Game in Washington, DC.	77
Figure 9.1	Bill Dickey (*far right*) poses with Hall of Famer Joe Cronin (*center*) and Lou Gehrig in 1937.	85
Figure 10.1	Longtime New York Giants manager John McGraw (*right*) poses with Babe Ruth, 1923.	94
Figure 10.2	Members of the New York Giants, a frequent nemesis of the Yankees during the 1920s and 1930s, mill around a batting cage, 1923.	96
Figure 11.1	Sportswriter Grantland Rice, 1920.	103
Figure 11.2	Postmaster General James A. Farley, shown in 1937, was among those who spoke on Lou Gehrig Appreciation Day.	108
Figure 11.3	Herb Pennock loosens up in 1913 as a member of the Philadelphia Athletics a decade before he would join the Yankees along with Lou Gehrig.	110

Figure 12.1	Lou Gehrig (*left*) and Babe Ruth (*right*), 1931. Gehrig was the luckiest man for, among other things, having spent a decade playing alongside Babe Ruth, considered by many to be the greatest player ever.	115
Figure 13.1	The Columbia University football team, presumably with Lou Gehrig in the huddle, competes on campus at Baker Field in 1922, as seen in an aerial photograph.	120
Figure 14.1	Fullback Lou Gehrig at Columbia University, ca. 1922.	130
Figure 15.1	One of the things Lou Gehrig had to live for was his budding relationship with New York City mayor Fiorello La Guardia, seen leaving the White House in 1938, the year before the mayor appointed Gehrig to the New York City Board of Parole.	140
Figure E.1	Babe Ruth shortly before the franchise-changing deal that sent him to the Yankees in 1920.	149
Figure E.2	Babe Ruth, in this instance a fan, attends a ball game, 1922.	153

PREFACE

The good die first,
And they whose hearts are dry as summer dust
Burn to the socket.

—William Wordsworth

This is the story of a famous speech, famous not because of what was said but because of the dire circumstances that faced Lou Gehrig when he calmly delivered it to tens of thousands of baseball fans at Yankee Stadium. To dissect the speech for this book, I dedicate each chapter to specific elements of what the slugger said that day: his references to the fans who paid to watch him play, even during the Great Depression; to the players who labored beside him on the field, many of them in his shadow; to his trusted field managers, whom he dearly loved; to the Yankees executives who paid him handsomely to ply his trade of swinging a baseball bat; to his loving parents, who raised him with integrity and a rigid set of moral standards; and to his quirky mother-in-law, who embraced him like a son. A quotation from the speech begins each chapter, indicating which of the sentences Gehrig spoke to his audience of fans will be analyzed therein. Throughout the book, in the main body copy, quotations from the speech are presented in italic text.

Over the years, various iterations of Lou Gehrig's speech, in which he memorably declared himself *"the luckiest man on the face of the earth,"* have been proffered, and each has been accepted as gospel despite slight differences between them. The National Baseball Hall of Fame posts one version; LouGehrig.com, another; and still others abound. The truth is that no one knows for certain what Gehrig said in totality on that summer day in 1939. Only four sentences captured on film have survived, and no complete audio recording of the speech is known to exist.

The narrative I follow is the most accurate reconstruction of that speech available. It was compiled from incomplete audio as well as articles published by the two wire services and most of the major newspapers that existed in and around New York City at that time, most of which long ago shuttered their doors and whose archive of articles has largely been forgotten. These include United Press International (UPI), the Associated Press (AP), the *New York Times*, the *Washington Post*, the *New York Daily News*, the *New York Sun*, the *New York Post*, the *New York Daily Mirror*, the *New York Journal-American*, and the *New York Herald Tribune*. In reconstructing Gehrig's speech, I compared the wording of quotations in each original news account from publication to publication and assumed accuracy where the same quotations from different writers were similar and when certain catchphrases were used by two or more reporters. Much of this compilation reflects other long-accepted versions; however, words and phrases have been added where the historical record dictates.

Note that the vast majority of newspapers covering the speech ran wire service stories and neither UPI nor the AP quoted Gehrig extensively. Most writers paraphrased Gehrig's comments, and few used more than a couple quotations in their published accounts, one of them being the *New York Daily News*. As history has, I conferred greater accuracy upon the *Daily News*' Rosaleen Doherty, who was seated with Gehrig's wife and parents and who, as a professional journalist, would have been duty bound to confirm the accuracy of her note taking with Mrs. Gehrig if she had questions or doubts about what was said. To Doherty, several of whose quotations appear in long-accepted versions of Gehrig's speech, accurate note taking would have been a matter of professional pride. Additionally, her coverage was more extensive, and her use of quotation was more exhaustive than others'. In some instances her quotations were similar to those of other reporters; in other cases they were less so. Where a quotation resembled that penned by another reporter, the cadence of the wording was compared with portions of the speech captured on audio, and accuracy was assumed if the quotation being evaluated read as if Gehrig might have spoken it.

Here is a sentence-by-sentence breakdown of the speech, with Gehrig's presumed words in italics followed by bracketed notes on their source:

Fans, for the past two weeks you've been reading about a bad break. Today I consider myself the luckiest man on the face of the earth.[1]

[The salutation and the two sentences noted here were captured on video and are therefore accurate.]

I've been walking into ballparks for seventeen years and have never received anything but kindness and encouragement from you fans.

[There are several versions of this quotation, with some reporters writing "sixteen" and even "fifteen" years as the duration of Gehrig's career and some using "ball fields" and others "ballparks." This quotation is a compilation from multiple writers, the majority of whom used "ballparks," and is likely fairly accurate.]

Mine has been a full life.[2]

[Only one reporter, the *Washington Post*'s Shirley Povich, used this quotation. Even journalists who are slow note takers can accurately capture short quotations despite sometimes stumbling with longer ones, and Povich was one of the best. This comment is short enough for any journalist to report it without error—and Gehrig likely said it. No other known versions of Gehrig's speech carry this quotation, perhaps because of its seeming insignificance at the time.]

Newspapers have said nice things about me, which I found hard to believe myself.[3]

[Only the *New York Sun* used this quotation, and it's not probable that an experienced reporter for a major newspaper would have misreported a sentence that depicted Gehrig's relationship with that same media. No other known versions of Gehrig's speech carry this quotation.]

When you look around, wouldn't you consider it a privilege to associate yourself with such fine-looking men as are standing in uniform in this ballpark today?

[This is the third of four sentences captured on video and is accurate.]

Sure, I'm lucky.[4]

[This brief exclamation was reported by *New York Daily News* reporter Doherty, who was seated with Mrs. Gehrig and thus had additional pressure on her to accurately report Gehrig's words. The quotation is short and likely on the mark.]

Who wouldn't consider it an honor to have known Jacob Ruppert?

Also, the builder of baseball's greatest empire, Ed Barrow?

To have spent six years with such a grand little fellow as Miller Huggins?[5]

[These three sentences are from the *New York Daily News*.]

To have spent the next nine years with that master psychologist, the greatest manager in baseball today, Joe McCarthy?[6]

[The Associated Press and the *New York Daily News* were similar in their reporting of this comment. This compilation uses "greatest," as most writers did, rather than "best" or "smartest."]

And when you have the privilege of rooming, eating, playing cards, and knowing one of the greatest fellows that ever lived, my roommate, Bill Dickey.[7]

[Although certain traditional transcripts of Gehrig's speech omit any reference to Dickey, at least four reporters mentioned him in their accounts of the speech, so the reference is accurate. I went with this quotation from the *New York Herald Tribune* since thorough notes would have been required to compile such a complex quotation and it's unlikely that anything written here was not said. No previously accepted versions of Gehrig's speech carry this extensive a quotation.]

When the fellows from across the river, the New York Giants, a team you would give your right arm to beat, and vice versa, sends a gift, that's something.[8]

[The *New York Daily News* and the *Washington Post* used similar language. This quotation combines their narratives and is as accurate as possible.]

*It's something to be remembered by a rival organization.*⁹

[The *New York Post* was the only newspaper to use this sentence, which includes the uncommon descriptor "rival." The word is not likely to have been misreported; therefore, neither is the sentence itself. No other known versions of Gehrig's speech carry this quotation.]

*When the groundskeepers and office staff and writers and old timers and players and those boys in white coats all remember you with trophies, that's something.*¹⁰

[This quotation was reported with extensive disparity by several writers. Only the *Daily News* mentioned six different groups of people, and it's unlikely that any one of those six would have been noted if Gehrig hadn't mentioned that group. I went with Doherty's quotation, replacing "concessionaires," which others used, with "boys in white coats" because the latter term is too unusual to have been misreported.]

*When you have a mother-in-law who takes sides with you in squabbles against her own daughter—that's really something.*¹¹

[The Associated Press and the *Daily News* were again similar in their reporting. However, several reporters used "against" rather than "with," so this quotation is a slight compilation with that minor change added.]

*When you have a father and a mother who work all their lives so that you can have an education and build your body, it's a blessing.*¹²

[Again, the *Daily News*.]

*When you have a wonderful wife who has been a tower of strength show more courage than I ever dreamed existed—that's the finest thing I know.*¹³

[This sentence is a compilation that borrows from the *New York Post* and the *Daily News*, whose quotations were similar.]

So I close in saying that I might've been given a bad break, but I've got an awful lot to live for. Thank you.

[This is the final quotation captured on video and, like the other three, is accurate.]

A final note: in covering the same event, reporters from different media often quote a person using slightly different verbiage, as Eliot Asinof's book on the 1919 Black Sox scandal underscored. Asinof, writing in *Eight Men Out*, said Shoeless Joe Jackson's confession "was quoted four different ways by four different papers."[14] So it was with Gehrig's speech. Unless a complete audio recording of the speech is someday uncovered, it may never be known exactly what Gehrig said on that forlorn summer day. Until and unless that ever occurs, this new narrative will have to suffice as Gehrig's Bronx epitaph.

ACKNOWLEDGMENTS

In any book where baseball statistics play a role in describing vital characters or subject matter, it's essential to acknowledge the source of that data: in this case, the Baseball Reference website (baseball-reference.com) and the long-defunct *Baseball Encyclopedia*. Much of the statistical data contained herein were provided by these numerical giants, and I'm grateful for the efforts of their tireless staff.

The hook to any manuscript is the cover photograph, and *Bronx Epitaph* is no exception. The photograph of Gehrig wiping tears from his eyes is perhaps the most definitive image of his famous farewell speech. The photo was shot by Murray Becker of the Associated Press, who had captured an iconic image of the burning Hindenburg two years earlier. For the AP's cooperation in making the photograph available, and to Tricia Gesner and AP Images for facilitating its use, I'm thankful.

Other photographs also were essential in the creation of this book. No cultural institution more dependably makes available rare photographs than the Library of Congress. Specifically, thanks go to the Harris & Ewing Collection, the George Grantham Bain Collection, the National Photo Company Collection, and the Adams & Grace Company, whose photos are all made available free of charge and without copyright restriction through the Library of Congress.

Another reliable source of photography was Erin Beasley at the Smithsonian Institute's National Portrait Gallery. For providing a photograph of Mr. Gehrig standing alongside Babe Ruth, I offer my gratitude.

A final photograph, of Mr. Gehrig wearing his Columbia University baseball uniform, is housed at Columbia University and is now in the public domain. I'm appreciative of the university, its library, and the photographer, whose identity is unknown.

In compiling a book of this nature, I borrow from other authors, and each is attributed in the text where appropriate. They include Eleanor Gehrig and Joseph Durso, Frank Graham, Ray Robinson, Jonathan Eig, Steve Steinberg and Lyle Spatz, Daniel Levitt, and Harvey Frommer. Their research, added to my own, was indispensable.

Perhaps most difficult was deciding which version of Gehrig's speech to use. In evaluating that, I decided to enlist the help of many authors—those erstwhile newspaper scribes who covered the event on July 4, 1939. Each had their own take on what was said, and in many cases similar quotations differed decidedly in their eventual wording, making it difficult to ascribe true accuracy. Based upon my news instincts, which I used to determine the likely reliability of each quotation, I came up with my own version of the speech. It is similar to many others that have been offered through the years, including those provided by the National Baseball Hall of Fame and Museum, LouGehrig.com, and others, although mine includes minimal wording heretofore not put forward as gospel.

Finally, thanks, too, to the many players, all of them former Yankees, who contributed their opinions on Lou Gehrig's important legacy. Without their participation it would have been impossible to paint a thorough portrait of Gehrig and the Yankees organization. Included are the following players:

- Bobby Shantz, 1952 American League Most Valuable Player with the Philadelphia Athletics. Shantz was 24–7 that season with a 2.48 ERA and twenty-seven complete games and was named to the All-Star team for a second time. A Yankee from 1957–60, Shantz, now ninety-seven, was an excellent fielding pitcher who won eight consecutive Gold Glove awards between 1957 and 1964.

- Bill Virdon, 1955 National League Rookie of the Year with the St. Louis Cardinals. Virdon later played ten seasons with the Pittsburgh Pirates and eventually managed the Yankees, Pirates, Houston Astros, and Montreal Expos. Virdon, who was preparing to bat when Bill Mazeroski hit his World Series–winning home run in 1960, was named Manager of the Year in 1974, his only full season with the Yankees.

- Irv Noren, an All-Star with the Yankees in 1954. Noren played eleven seasons in the major leagues, five of them with the

Yankees, and as a center fielder was the bridge between the recently retired Joe DiMaggio and injured Mickey Mantle. His best season was 1950, when the rookie hit fourteen home runs, drove in ninety-eight runners, and batted .295. He died twenty-two days after I interviewed him for this book.

- Rick Dempsey, who played twenty-four seasons in the major leagues—four of them with the Yankees. Dempsey was a key member of the 1988 Los Angeles Dodgers team that was sparked to a world championship by Kirk Gibson's iconic ninth-inning home run in game one.

- Andy McGaffigan, who played with five teams during a highly respectable career. McGaffigan compiled an impressive 3.38 ERA over eleven seasons in the major leagues.

- Roger Repoz, who played nine seasons in the big leagues—three of them with the Yankees. Repoz was hailed as a budding star in the mold of Mickey Mantle when he broke in with the Yankees in 1964.

- Greg Cadaret, who played ten seasons in the major leagues—three of them with the Yankees. Playing for eight teams, Cadaret compiled a 3.99 ERA.

- Mike Buddie, who played two seasons with the Yankees and five years overall. In 2019, in a clear acknowledgment of his baseball acumen, Buddie was named athletic director at West Point.

- Gil Patterson, who pitched one season in the big leagues, that with the Yankees. After injuring his pitching arm, Patterson underwent eight operations and was out of baseball for two years. However, he fought back, taught himself to throw left-handed, and eventually was able to pitch professionally both right- and left-handed. Despite his brief major-league career, Patterson persisted within the organization to become the Oakland A's minor-league pitching coordinator, a position he has held since 2015.

- Fred Kipp, who pitched four seasons in the major leagues, his final one with the Yankees. Though a pitcher, Kipp's claim to fame was as a hitter. As a Dodger in 1958, Kipp was nine for thirty-six, for a .250 batting average, outstanding for a pitcher. He never recorded a hit in any of his other brief major-league seasons.

    I'd also like to acknowledge Richard Carlin, senior acquisitions editor at the State University of New York Press, for including *Bronx Epitaph* among its Excelsior Editions publications. Without the tireless work of a top-flight publisher and its staff, a manuscript is only a stack of paper. SUNY Press made the project one that I'm proud of.

    Finally, I'm grateful to Vinnie Anella, who as a youngster was present that day for Gehrig's fabled speech and is very much alive today. Anella's reminiscences give us a rare window into that memorable day, if only for a quick glimpse. Few people are alive today who are fortunate to recall that moment from personal experience, and one of them is Anella, now eighty-nine. I'm appreciative to him for sharing his fading recollections, providing a rare treat while helping to resurrect, for the first time in book form, Gehrig's Bronx epitaph.

INTRODUCTION

His speech was a baseball moment that had nothing to do with playing. It was baseball's Gettysburg Address.

—Marty Appel, baseball historian

Fans, for the past two weeks you've been reading about a bad break. Today I consider myself the luckiest man on the face of the earth. I've been walking into ballparks for seventeen years and have never received anything but kindness and encouragement from you fans. Mine has been a full life. Newspapers have said nice things about me, which I found hard to believe myself. When you look around, wouldn't you consider it a privilege to associate yourself with such fine-looking men as are standing in uniform in this ballpark today? Sure, I'm lucky. Who wouldn't consider it an honor to have known Jacob Ruppert? Also, the builder of baseball's greatest empire, Ed Barrow? To have spent six years with such a grand little fellow as Miller Huggins? To have spent the next nine years with that master psychologist, the greatest manager in baseball today, Joe McCarthy? And when you have the privilege of rooming, eating, playing cards, and knowing one of the greatest fellows that ever lived, my roommate, Bill Dickey. When the fellows from across the river, the New York Giants, a team you would give your right arm to beat, and vice versa, sends a gift, that's something. It's something to be remembered by a rival organization. When the groundskeepers and office staff and writers and old timers and players and those boys in white coats all remember you with trophies, that's something. When

> *you have a mother-in-law who takes sides with you in squabbles against her own daughter—that's really something. When you have a father and a mother who work all their lives so that you can have an education and build your body, it's a blessing. When you have a wonderful wife who has been a tower of strength show more courage than I ever dreamed existed—that's the finest thing I know. So I close in saying that I might've been given a bad break, but I've got an awful lot to live for. Thank you.*

The man in baggy pinstripes stared plaintively down at the Yankee Stadium turf, like a hitter facing long odds with a game hanging in the balance. Like a man facing death. The illusory focus of Lou Gehrig's awkward gaze, his eyes descending, face grim, was something dark, like the mood of the 61,808 fans in attendance that day, July 4, 1939, as the fabled New York Yankees, who would win the World Series that season, prepared to take on the lowly Washington Senators in the second game of a doubleheader.

As noir author Mike Roscoe proclaimed in the title of his book, death is a round black ball, and Gehrig knew plenty about round balls—white ones with red seams, each representing new hope as it zoomed toward his sizzling bat at high speed. After all, in seventeen seasons as a major-league ballplayer, he had swatted plenty of balls around various major-league parks: 2,721 of them for hits, 534 for doubles, 163 for triples, and 493 for home runs. Gehrig's lifetime batting average of .340 ranks sixteenth on the all-time list of major-league career leaders.

In sports parlance, Gehrig was a "baseball great," except for that 1939 season when something went terribly wrong and he relegated himself to the Yankees bench en route to hitting an unfathomable .143—that, after driving in 114 runs the previous year.

On the nation's 163rd birthday, Gehrig had come to a place where he didn't want to be: Yankee Stadium. He stood at a spot where he didn't want to stand: near home plate. He spoke to a crowd whom he didn't want to address. Those listening didn't want to hear what their hero had to say, either, not on that day. For Gehrig—the Iron Horse, Larrupin' Lou, Buster Pants, Locomotive Lou—had come to say goodbye, to a Hall of Fame career, to the fans who had supported him since the year that Yankee Stadium opened, to his cherished teammates, and effectively to life itself. On that day he was facing a round, black ball.

Introduction | 3

Figure I.1. Lou Gehrig at Columbia University, ca. 1923. Columbia University.

Though dressed in familiar Yankees pinstripes with the number four blazoned on the back, surrounded by celebratory bunting and looking fit enough to start the afternoon game at first base, Gehrig would not play baseball again; he was replaced at his position by Babe Dahlgren, who decades later would die in Arcadia, California, my hometown. As he stood at home plate surrounded by members of the legendary 1927 Yankees as well as his contemporary 1939 teammates, some of the game's most accomplished on-field executives, and other dedicated Yankees employees, with trophies and gifts propped delicately at his feet, Gehrig, the idol of New York, faced a veritable death sentence. He had 698 days to live.

Those generous remembrances fit the man, the event, the mood. They included a silver service set from Yankees management; two silver platters and a silver pitcher from the Harry M. Stevens company, the ball club's concessionaire; a fishing pole and assorted tackle from the team's ushers and employees; a silver loving cup from the team's office staff; a pair of silver candlesticks and a fruit bowl from the crosstown rival, the New York Giants; a tobacco stand presented by the Baseball Writers' Association of America, several of whose members covered the team; scrolls from fans of the Washington Senators; a parchment from the Old Timers Association of Denver; a ring from Dieges & Clust, the makers of Gehrig's 1927 and 1936 World Series rings; and, perhaps most meaningful to the slugger, a silver trophy graced with an eagle, presented by Gehrig's teammates. Inscribed on the trophy were the names of each player along with a poem written by sportswriter John Kieran of the *New York Times*, a favorite scribe of Yankees players and Gehrig's neighbor and close friend. The poem, requested by Gehrig's roommate, Dickey, read,

To LOU GEHRIG

We've been to the wars together;
We took our foes as they came:
And always you were the leader,
And ever you played the game.
Idol of cheering millions,
Records are yours by sheaves;
Iron of frame they hailed you;
Decked you with laurel leaves.
But higher than that we hold you,
We who have known you best;
Knowing the way you came through
Every human test.
Let this be a silent token
Of lasting friendship's gleam
And all that we've left unspoken.
Your Pals of the Yankee Team.[1]

Gehrig stood uncomfortably, hands clasped in front of him, toeing the dirt back and forth with his cleats, probably wishing the ground below would open up and collapse around him in a maw. As the revered slugger fought back tears, Babe Ruth, like Gehrig once a feared cog in the Yankees' famed Murderer's Row and a former roommate of his, spoke to the crowd, as did New York mayor Fiorello La Guardia, Postmaster General James A. Farley, and Yankees manager Joe McCarthy. Gehrig had indicated beforehand he did not wish to address the fans, and as sportswriter Sid Mercer, master of ceremonies for the event, told the restless crowd that Gehrig was too emotional to speak, it appeared as though the slugger's wish would be honored. As fate would have it, that wouldn't be the case. In this singular instance, swept up in emotion by a crowd that wanted to hear his voice, many for the first and last time, Gehrig became the unluckiest man on the face of the earth.

Those in the crowd had something entirely different in mind than Gehrig had. Rising to their feet, they began to wave fedoras and chant loudly in unison for their hero to speak. On that day, despite the emotion that wrung his soul, Gehrig *had* to speak—and his manager, McCarthy, a veteran of the Yankee wars, knew as much—for the ages. McCarthy prodded his star, patting him gently on the back and offering words of encouragement in an effort to steer the big first baseman toward the microphone against the player's wishes. McCarthy, who had earlier told the crowd "it was a sad day" when Gehrig told him he was quitting baseball,[2] succeeded. So, jaw clenched, chewing on a stick of gum likely provided by his usual supplier, team trainer Earle V. "Doc" Painter, rubbing his eyes, and speaking without the notes he had penned just the night before, Gehrig composed himself and began to talk, ever so reluctantly but with the same command and intensity he had exhibited on the baseball diamond so many times throughout his memorable career—until May 2, that is, when he broke the bad news to McCarthy that he was through, a decision that made more sense when the Mayo Clinic revealed to the Yankees seven weeks later that Gehrig had developed amyotrophic lateral sclerosis (ALS). Gehrig's speech was simple, eloquent, touching, memorable—and miraculous, given the emotion and futility that were etched on his face, pained but still youthful.

Watching from behind the Yankees dugout was his wife, Eleanor, who was seated with Gehrig's parents; her brother, Frank; and the wives of Yankees executive Ed Barrow and manager McCarthy. They were joined by *New York Daily News* reporter Rosaleen Doherty, who wrote that despite people openly sobbing all around her, Eleanor remained composed.

"I'm glad Lou was able to walk out there and make his little talk over the microphone," Eleanor said. "I knew he wouldn't let the fans down."[3]

After Gehrig finished his "little talk" and the crowd began to cheer for what seemed like an eternity, Ruth walked over and embraced his teammate, then said something that made him smile. For Gehrig, there would be few smiles during his final 698 days.

Eighty-four years later, what Gehrig said in his farewell speech remains to us as a paraphrase. There is no transcript, no complete sound recording exists, and only a snippet of film was preserved. The film that exists captured seventy short words, among them the most memorable ever uttered in a sports theater: "Today I consider myself the luckiest man on the face of the earth," a phrase that former Yankee Irv Noren, who played with the club from 1952 to 1956, put into unique perspective shortly before his own death. "It's pretty neat that he was able to say that in front of a lot of people who believed him," said Noren, who made the American League All-Star team in 1954, fifteen years after Gehrig retired. "I consider *myself* the luckiest man because although I'm ninety-five I still remember things."[4] Noren died three weeks later.

The rest of Gehrig's heart-rending oratory was compiled from news dispatches that varied by sportswriter; it encompasses 334 words, shorter than a letter home. Shorter than a codicil.

As speeches go, his "Luckiest Man" discourse was classic Gehrig—sweet, humble, incontrovertible in its message and simplicity. Only eighty-four words longer than the Gettysburg Address, it has withstood the test of time. Few speeches have resonated as poignantly. President Abraham Lincoln's battlefield oration, delivered in South Central Pennsylvania on November 19, 1863, did. So did President Franklin Roosevelt's Pearl Harbor address to Congress on December 8, 1941. And Martin Luther King Jr.'s "I Have a Dream" speech, presented in Washington, DC, on August 28, 1963. In the history of sports, no speech reverberates more resoundingly than Gehrig's brief dialogue.

Henry Louis Gehrig was born on June 19, 1903, at 1994 Second Avenue in an Upper East Side section of Manhattan known as Yorkville. His parents were Heinrich and Christina Gehrig, German immigrants who had moved to the area shortly before their son was born. From the beginning the Gehrigs strove to ensure that their young boy would succeed, although his father had difficulty finding employment as a metal worker. That, combined with the senior Gehrig's chronic ill health, made things challenging for the Gehrig family, and Mrs. Gehrig eventually took on miscellaneous jobs, including cooking for wealthy New York residents, laundering, and house cleaning, in hopes of balancing the household budget;

she also managed the family home, more so after her husband became disabled. Although facing other difficulties along the way, including the deaths of Lou Gehrig's unnamed infant brother and two young sisters, the family somehow managed to survive.

The Gehrigs moved several times after the future ballplayer's birth, eventually residing at Amsterdam Avenue and 170th Street near a ballpark where the old New York Highlanders, predecessor to the Yankees, played. From his earliest days the boy was inundated with sports, including football, gymnastics, soccer, and, of course, baseball. While his father insisted he strengthen his body, Lou Gehrig's mother demanded their son receive a good education. He accepted both of their good wishes and hoped to become an engineer.

"You must study," Mrs. Gehrig said.[5]

"He must play, too," Mr. Gehrig added.[6]

While her husband continued to struggle at times, Mrs. Gehrig was committed to making sure that their boy received an education, which he did. After attending Public School 132, he enrolled at the High School of Commerce in 1917, where he excelled in athletics—especially baseball and football. At first he declined to play on the baseball team because he was shy about appearing in front of crowds. However, with encouragement from his coach, the youth finally gave in and agreed to play. He was positioned at first base after demonstrating control issues as a pitcher and a lack of coordination in the outfield.

Despite those shortcomings, it was at Commerce, established the year before Gehrig's birth, where people first began to recognize his ability to play baseball, especially after he led his team to the New York State Baseball Championship and the inter-city championship game in Chicago. Gehrig's ninth-inning grand slam during the final game in the Windy City sewed up the title for Commerce, resulting in a tumultuous reception when the players returned home to New York by train. By virtue of his momentous home run, Gehrig, whose family had by then moved to 2079 Eighth Avenue in the same Yorkville neighborhood, was all everyone talked about, and the reception was his first intersection with fan adoration.

After graduating from the High School of Commerce in 1921, Gehrig attracted the attention of the New York Giants, who offered him a tryout that he eventually failed despite hitting six consecutive home runs. He was down and nearly out, but the indomitable Gehrig recovered and continued forging ahead with his new dream, that of becoming a professional baseball player.

Setting baseball aside at least for the moment, Gehrig enrolled at Columbia University in 1921 under a football scholarship. The fit was a good one, as Gehrig's parents were employed, according to varying accounts, at either the Sigma Nu or Phi Delta Theta fraternity on campus, Mr. Gehrig as a handyman and his wife as a cook; while in high school, the younger Gehrig helped out during dinners. In fact, a fraternity brother who remembered Gehrig as his graduation from Commerce came into view was instrumental in securing his enrollment at the Ivy League school after learning of the young man's prowess as an athlete. Once there, Gehrig played fullback on the football team, showing excellent form. He also joined the baseball team as a pitcher and first baseman, once striking out seventeen players in a game and earning the sobriquet "Columbia Lou." Gehrig was so good in college that he drew the attention of a Yankees scout, and in April 1923—the same month that Yankee Stadium opened—the team signed him to his first professional baseball contract. For nothing more than autographing a piece of paper, something he would do often over the subsequent seventeen years, Gehrig received a $1,500 bonus—significant spondulix during the Roaring Twenties, and his family's ticket out of Yorkville. The future Larrupin' Lou was on his way.

After signing with the eventual Bronx Bombers, Gehrig left college in 1923 and joined the Yankees' minor-league club in Hartford, Connecticut, playing in the Eastern League. It was there that he hit a lofty .304 during his only season in the minor leagues—good enough to earn him a trip up to the big leagues.

"We were mighty short on infielders in those days," the big first baseman modestly said years later, intimating it was that shortage that enabled him to reach the major leagues.[7] It was not.

His early seasons in the majors were disappointing, even though his statistics—although sparse—were acceptable. During his first season with the ball club, Gehrig was largely used as a pinch hitter, and he performed capably at the plate, hitting well over .400 with a home run in twenty-nine at bats. His reward was even fewer at bats in 1924, when he hit .500—six for twelve. While his offense had been limited to just forty-one at bats during his first two seasons as a Yankee, by 1925 his name would for the first time enter the conversation for the American League Most Valuable Player (MVP) Award.

For Gehrig, everything was happening with head-spinning speed: a short "season" at Columbia University, an even shorter one with the Hartford Senators, then a brief learning curve with the Yankees before settling in as a star playing alongside his heroes, including the legendary Ruth. Over the next few seasons Gehrig would mature as both a person and a player, and by 1927 he was recognized as a solid member of the feared Murderers' Row and an indispensable cog in one of the finest teams ever compiled.

In 1925, his first season as a regular position player, Gehrig hit an impressive .295 with twenty home runs and sixty-eight RBI. After that there was no holding back the quiet New Yorker: he hit .313 with sixteen home runs in 1926, .373 with forty-seven home runs in his 1927 MVP season (at that time, players were only allowed to win the award once), .374 with twenty-seven home runs in 1928, .300 with thirty-five home runs in 1929, .379 with forty-one home runs in 1930, and .341 with forty-six home runs in 1931.

"Irrespective of any other players on our club, I am the man to whom the team looks as a pacesetter," he once said. "Every year I am told I am the hitter who must lead the Yankees to the pennant. That suits me fine."[8] It is not known what slugging leader Babe Ruth thought of the comment.

Perhaps the player's greatest individual accomplishment occurred during his tenth season with the club, in 1932, when Gehrig, whom the late *Los Angeles Times* sports columnist Jim Murray once described as "a symbol of indestructibility—a Gibraltar in cleats,"[9] recorded the finest game of his exceptionally fine career. The game, a 20–13 drubbing of the Philadelphia Athletics in front of the A's home fans, would mark him forever as one of the greatest ballplayers the game has ever known. On that day Gehrig slugged four home runs and narrowly missed a fifth, becoming the first player in the modern era and the first in the history of the American League to achieve the feat.

There were other highlights during his long and illustrious career: two MVP awards (1927 and 1936), one batting crown (1934), a Triple Crown the same season, seven times an All-Star (1933 through 1939—the All-Star Game did not originate until its creation in concert with the Chicago World's Fair in 1933, ten years after Gehrig's career began), home-run leader three times (1931, 1934, and 1936), and RBI leader five times (1927, 1928, 1930, 1931, and 1934). At one time or another he also led the American League in hits, doubles, triples, on-base percentage, and slugging percentage.

Still, Gehrig's four-home-run game indisputably elevates him above most ballplayers of his or any other era. Ruth, who for decades was the major-league career home run leader, never accomplished the feat. Neither did Hank Aaron, the man who surpassed Ruth, nor Barry Bonds, who succeeded the great Aaron. Others who never hit four home runs during a single game include Ted Williams, Mickey Mantle, Ernie Banks, Mel Ott, and Joe DiMaggio.

Even more important than his on-field legacy is the speech, which elevates the man to an almost mythical stature. Ballplayers have been playing and retiring from the game for 150 years, sometimes holding press conferences to announce their departure, other times delivering brief statements or press releases to announce their superannuation, and still other times making no public gesture whatsoever. Few have departed with the dignity and courage displayed by Gehrig, who likely would have preferred to avoid Yankee Stadium altogether on Independence Day 1939. After all, he hadn't played in months, the announcement of his ALS had been made, there were few expectations of him as either a player or a representative of the Yankees organization as their season reached the halfway point, and his denouement was settled. A day honoring—indeed, memorializing—Gehrig may have been the last thing he wanted as his life began to fade into immortality.

"It took a lot of courage," said the late Yankee star Noren, Mantle's one-time road roommate. "He meant what he said."[10]

A perfect man might have relished an opportunity to bid farewell to those who had supported him for so many years, but Gehrig wasn't perfect. A strange mixture of confidence and insecurity, he was frugal yet displayed great generosity when so moved. He was affable yet moody and was still closely attached to his mother, although he easily switched his devotion to the woman he would marry, the socialite Eleanor Twitchell. He wrote poignant letters, wiped away tears when his wife read passages from literature, and won a ribbon after entering his dog in a local show; the dog, named Afra, was a breed of—what else?—German shepherd. Gehrig even played the lead role in the long-forgotten movie *Rawhide*, the only true all-star in a less-than-all-star cast.[11]

Why did Gehrig address his speech only to the fans when others were lined up along the infield to bid him goodbye? Why did he acknowledge those whom he named in the speech, including the Yankees general manager Barrow, the owner Ruppert, former field manager Huggins, current manager McCarthy, and the catcher Dickey? Why did he acknowledge the New York Giants, of all teams? And his mother-in-law, Nellie Mulvaney Twitchell? What about the groundskeepers, office staff, concessionaires, and, especially, the sportswriters, some of whom were less than friendly to him toward the end of his career—why were they referenced? And why did he consider himself lucky while facing a dreadful death?

The answers to those questions are inferred in responses to his death by those who either knew Gehrig or wished they had. One sportswriter described him as "the gamest guy I ever saw."[12] When Gehrig passed away, a tearful Ruth, who had not been close to the slugger for several years, rushed to his home, as did a shaken Barrow. Across town, McCarthy and his players were, like Barrow, stunned and distraught. Dickey, Gehrig's closest friend, wept. Before long, automobiles lined the street in front of the home where Gehrig had spent his dying days wasting away. As a tribute to its fallen hero, flags across New York City flew at half-staff.

For nineteen years Gehrig was a beloved Yankee—seventeen as a player and two as a casualty of life. He seldom missed a game, hit home runs when the team needed them most, and helped lead the Yankees to eight World Series titles. Then, suddenly, he was gone forever. His legacy? A preponderance of impressive statistics, one major-league record that stood for decades (most career grand slams), one American League record that still stands (most RBI in a season), one four-home-run game, twice hitting for the cycle, and a speech for the ages.

Bronx Epitaph is a window into Lou Gehrig's rich, full life, viewed through the cataract of his "Luckiest Man" speech. Voiced by a player who was peerless at what he did, the speech defines the man in conflicting terms. Gehrig likely saw himself as others did: exceedingly lucky and blessed with good parents, a loving wife, limitless fame, outstanding health, a Corinthian attitude, and abilities far beyond those of most mortal men. Toward the end, however, the picture changed dramatically. After two years away from baseball, his familiarity among New Yorkers had begun to diminish, his physicality had departed, and all that was left was a shell of what Gehrig once represented—his parents, wife, and winning attitude notwithstanding. Perhaps the writer Steven Goldman put it best: "Lou Gehrig didn't have a great deal of luck in the end."[13]

Today, with that ending a part of baseball history, there's an unmistakable certainty: the revered Iron Horse's famous speech was one for the ages.

CHAPTER 1

FANS

> I've been walking into ballparks for seventeen years and have never received anything but kindness and encouragement from you fans. Mine has been a full life.
>
> —Lou Gehrig, "Luckiest Man" speech

Like a wraith, the shapely nymph drifted in through the floodlit night. And sometimes during the day. For years she dashed across baseball theaters from coast to coast, eliciting notice from media co-conspirators. To many, including ballpark police, she was baseball's fan from Sheol. To others, depending upon their perspective, she was heavenly.

Like most people, she had two names, but only one really mattered: Morganna. Her surname, Roberts, was irrelevant, and so she is today despite her bathycolpian figure. Her nickname? The Kissing Bandit.

Morganna's method of operating was simple: kiss the boys and make them sigh. It all began in 1969 when the Louisville hugger rushed onto the turf at Crosley Field in Cincinnati and parked a buss on Reds infielder Pete Rose. From there, she quietly moved on to New York Mets pitcher Nolan Ryan, Cincinnati Reds catcher Johnny Bench, Los Angeles Dodgers first baseman Steve Garvey, and Baltimore Orioles shortstop Cal Ripken Jr. Kansas City Royals third baseman George Brett was a favorite—Morganna kissed him twice. She seemed to have a proclivity for Hall of Famers. It wasn't the kiss that stirred fans so much as it was the vision, this comely faro racing over the diamond toward her coveted man-prize. To baseball fans, she was the "it girl" of 1969.

A darker side of fandom was displayed seven years later, on April 25, 1976. On that date, a father and his young son rushed onto the outfield grass at Dodger Stadium and, while crouched on the turf, attempted to ignite an American flag. Dodgers right fielder Rick Monday came to the rescue, racing across the field like a cavalry soldier to grab the banner before it burst into a red glare and trotting it toward the infield. The interlopers were escorted off the playing field—never, it seems, to be heard from again. Monday, on a Sunday, was a one-day hero.

Years later, Dodgers second baseman Steve Sax had his own memorable interaction with fans upon developing an inexplicable "syndrome" that gave rise to the nickname Scatter Arm Sax. It began in 1983 when Sax became enigmatically unable to accurately throw over to first base on routine ground balls, committing a whopping thirty errors on the season. As the syndrome spun out of control, fans seated behind first base wore batting helmets as tongue-in-cheek protection. Teammate Pedro Guerrero, an outfielder who had recently been shifted from his outfield comfort zone and over to third base, was once asked his first thought whenever he played the infield. "I hope they don't hit it to me," Guerrero said, smiling. When asked what his second thought was, he replied, "I hope they don't hit it to Sax."[1] Fortunately for Sax and wary fans seated behind the first-base dugout, by 1991 the yips were largely out of his system, and the five-time All-Star committed just seven errors in 724 fielding opportunities that season, ranking him among the top-fielding second basemen in the American League.

In baseball, it's all about the fans, short for *fanatics*. They fill stadiums; root, root, root for the home team; and help to pay a franchise's formidable bills, including player salaries. Mostly, they support the players. Sometimes they don't. Booed by fans, first baseman Dick Allen of the Philadelphia Phillies began scrawling letters on the infield dirt with his cleats: the word *boo* (representing boos and other abuse that the fans dished out), *October 2* (the date the Phillies' 1969 season would end and Allen would presumably and mercifully depart the team for good), *Coke* (because Allen wanted to hit a home run over the Coca-Cola sign to shut fans up), and *Why?* and *No* when Commissioner Bowie Kuhn ordered him to stop his infield antics.

On the flip side there was Lou Gehrig, a beloved Yankee who appreciated New York fans like nobody else. They, in turn, worshipped him. Perhaps that's why he addressed his epic speech to, simply, "*fans*," declaring he had "*never received anything but kindness and encouragement from you fans.*" The fans were his champions, and he seldom disappointed them.

Figure 1.1. Babe Ruth signs his autograph for fans at Griffith Stadium in Washington, DC, in 1937, two years after retiring. Library of Congress, Harris & Ewing Collection.

"He must have played pretty well to play as long as he did," said Bobby Shantz, who was the 1952 American League Most Valuable Player as a pitcher for the Philadelphia Athletics.[2]

It wasn't always that way, Gehrig's love affair with New York Yankees fans. As a student at the High School of Commerce, circa 1919, the muscular yet shy Gehrig at first wanted nothing to do with playing prep baseball. He feared playing in front of fans, many of whom were classmates.

Gehrig's friends were well aware of his ability to play sports, and they encouraged him to try out for the school's various teams. While his fear of fans and lack of confidence that he could succeed on the ball field inhibited him, in time his friends went behind his back and urged the teachers to convince Gehrig to put his talents on display for the good of Commerce. He eventually complied under threat of academic failure.

"Some of the kids had told my bookkeeping teacher that I could hit the ball a mile in the park," he once said. "The teacher ordered me to show up for a school game. I went up to the stadium on a streetcar. When I got there and saw so many people going into the field and heard all the cheering and noise, I was so scared I couldn't see straight. I turned right around and got back on the streetcar and went home. The next day the teacher threatened to flunk me if I didn't show up for the next game. So I went."[3]

It was fortunate for the sport of baseball and indeed for the entire world that Gehrig didn't let his youthful discomfort with playing in front of screaming fans deter him from engaging in baseball and, ultimately, succeeding far beyond his wildest dreams. By his senior year, Gehrig, by then confident, had led his team to the coveted inter-city baseball title in Chicago, defeating Lane Technical High School in a game at Cubs Park, which later would be known by another name: Wrigley Field. Fans or no fans, he was on his way to baseball stardom.

Fast forward two decades and Gehrig's relationship with fans had warmed considerably. That was evident on the day he gave his "Luckiest Man" speech, July 4, 1939. Slumping badly since the season had begun and physically unable to provide the team with any meaningful sock on offense, he had retired abruptly on May 2 after batting less than his weight—way less. His physical movements were off-kilter, he knew something was medically wrong, the media had suspected it as well, and as a result the fans were also concerned. Rather than continue to hobble his teammates as they worked to wrest another World Series title away from the competition, Gehrig stepped away from the game for good, ending his streak after having played in a record 2,130 consecutive games, a streak that began fourteen years earlier when he pinch-hit for Pee-Wee Wanninger on June 1, 1925. Gehrig, the man who seemed invincible, would become invisible—never to play baseball again, although his competitive spirit would live on from generation to generation of Yankees players.

"[Gehrig's winning attitude] carried over to the guys who were playing when I came up—Mickey Mantle, Roger Maris, Whitey Ford, and all the superstars," said Roger Repoz, an outfielder and first baseman with the Yankees from 1964 to 1966. "It carried over to us."[4]

Certainly, fans can be fickle, often supporting whoever is playing good baseball at a given moment. When things are going well, they cheer like a best friend. When things are going poorly, they boo like a worst enemy. For Gehrig in 1939, things were going poorly. At that point in the still-young season, sensing the physical hardships he was facing, few fans held it against him.

Unbeknownst to most people, Lou Gehrig Appreciation Day was originally planned to honor little-known Johnny Welaj. As such, Yankee Stadium hosted a modest ceremony on the identical spot—home plate—where Gehrig's gifts would be set in place later on that day.

Who was Johnny Welaj? Welaj was a rookie outfielder whose first year in the major leagues was shaping up nicely, and he'd continue to have success throughout 1939: on the year, Welaj would hit .274 in 201 at bats with the Washington Senators; during his short career he would record a "lifetime" batting average of .250 with four home runs and seventy-four RBI (see table A.4 in the appendix).

To the Manville, New Jersey, faithful, it was first and foremost Johnny Welaj Appreciation Day at Yankee Stadium, and the Moss Creek, Pennsylvania, native and Jersey transplant would forever recollect that it was secondarily Lou Gehrig Appreciation Day. In fact, when his own ceremony began, Welaj had no idea that Gehrig's famous retirement event would be held later that afternoon at the same spot within Yankee Stadium.

While Welaj invited scores of friends and relatives to his special day in the House that Ruth Built, the Gehrig entourage included only Eleanor and a handful of others. As the afternoon unfolded, just how the event would play out was somewhat uncertain, although one thing soon became clear: Gehrig's fans wanted him to speak, perhaps because they understood it would be his only opportunity to talk directly to them. He, on the other hand, was overcome with emotion and indicated he did not wish to say anything to the crowd. Nevertheless, wanting to hear from their hero, the fans took things into their own hands, waving hats, cheering, and chanting that they wanted him to speak. By the time he finally relented and stepped to the mic to begin talking, the cheers had risen to a crescendo. They died to a hush just as quickly when Gehrig began his epic speech, and the result was breathtaking. Fans, both men and women, teared up. Members of the media, some of them also his fans, also wept.

"You talk about sadness," the late, great *Washington Post* sportswriter Shirley Povich said in a televised interview half a century later. "That's the day I saw photographers cry." He added, "[Gehrig received] an ovation like I've never heard in my life before or since. It was the greatest thing I've ever seen."[5] That sadness was felt keenly by the legendary broadcaster Mel Allen, who was seated in the press box that day as a representative of his college newspaper. Calling Gehrig a tremendous guy, he said tears ran down his face as he listened to the big man speak.

Figure. 1.2. Brooklyn Dodgers fans voice their enthusiasm during the 1916 World Series. Library of Congress, George Grantham Bain Collection.

Over Gehrig's seventeen seasons in Yankees pinstripes, he performed in many ballparks. Yankee Stadium, where he played well and the fans worshipped him, had to be his favorite. The numerous others included the Polo Grounds, where the Yankees played before Yankee Stadium became their permanent venue and home of the New York Giants from 1891 to 1957, and Fenway Park, where the Boston Red Sox continue to play. He also played in Griffith Stadium, the Washington Senators' home field from 1911 to 1965, and Comiskey Park, where the White Sox played from 1910 until 1990.

For Gehrig, the wonderful fan treatment he was accustomed to receiving probably began around 1922, when those attending the baseball games at Columbia University began calling him "Columbia Lou." The nickname was apparently spawned when the young pitcher/outfielder displayed a proclivity for striking out batters.

Sandwiched between Gehrig's fan-fearful High School of Commerce days and his famous speech in front of nearly 62,000 chanting supporters were many instances of fan support. One of the first was in April 1923, when Gehrig homered three times in two games under the watchful eye of a Yankees scout. As he gleefully circled the bases following one blast at Columbia University's South Field, fans jumped from the stands, hoisted him onto their shoulders, and carried him away to the Columbia dressing room, which was situated in the school's Furnald Hall basement. In hot pursuit was the scout, who fought his way through the horde of delighted fans.

The following season, after signing with the Yankees, Gehrig stood at home plate with his manager, Miller Huggins, swatting balls over the outfield fence during his first batting practice. Suddenly, a voice from a nearby box was heard imploring him to hit another out of the park and show the slugging Babe Ruth how home runs should be hit. "Looks like he brought his own cheering section with him," his teammate Bob Meusel mused about the fan from a spot nearby.[6]

By 1925, when Gehrig was the Yankees' regular first baseman, he had already begun to attract a fan following, and most were delighted when he became a mainstay in the lineup. Once, when a neighbor had him hauled down to the local police station for playing baseball in the street with neighborhood children, a police lieutenant confessed his support for the player when he learned the man standing in front of him was none other than the famous Yankees first baseman. Admitting he had watched him play at Yankee Stadium the previous day, the officer praised Gehrig as a wonderful ballplayer and asked to shake his hand. Gehrig happily complied.

During the late 1920s, Gehrig and Ruth went head-to-head as elite home-run hitters, Mr. Clean versus the sultan of beer, hot dogs, and long dingers. In contrast to the already-legendary Ruth, Gehrig could have been a fan favorite by default. He wasn't—he earned it through hard work. Hitting third in the lineup for the Yankees, between 1927 and 1930 Ruth slugged sixty, fifty-four, forty-six, and forty-nine home runs for a total of 209. Gehrig, hitting cleanup, swatted forty-seven, twenty-seven, thirty-five, and forty-one home runs for a total of 150. During those four years, Gehrig hit fifty-nine fewer home runs while living a clean life compared with Ruth's beer-drinking, hot-dog-gulping lifestyle. However, he tied Ruth in runs batted in during the same period, with 618. While the two were coequals in run production, many fans preferred the modest Gehrig, whereas the writers liked the colorful, personable, highly quotable Ruth, although Gehrig also appealed to the baseball scribes just as Ruth appealed to fans. "It was . . . Gehrig who was getting the publicity, becoming a fan favorite and a media darling," wrote Harvey Frommer, author of *Five O'Clock Lightning* and a leading authority on Yankees baseball.[7]

Gehrig became even more of a fan favorite on June 3, 1932, when he knocked four balls out of Shibe Park in Philadelphia in a game against the Athletics. No American League player and no player in the modern era had ever accomplished this feat, and the achievement embedded Gehrig in the hearts of fans—even Athletics fans. "The Philadelphia fans, who were notorious Yankee haters, gave Gehrig a standing ovation as he crossed the plate" following his fourth home run, wrote James Lincoln Ray for the Society for American Baseball Research.[8]

As always, Gehrig responded modestly. After the game he hugged the great Ruth, under whose shadow he had labored for a good portion of his brilliant career. "There will never be another guy like the Babe," Gehrig said, characteristically minimizing his feat and deflecting attention away from himself. "I get more kick from seeing him hit one than I do from hitting one myself."[9]

Unfortunately for Gehrig, his performance didn't make as big a splash with the news media as it might have. The same day, legendary Giants manager John McGraw announced his retirement from baseball after thirty years at the helm, overshadowing Gehrig's accomplishment on the pages of sports sections around the country.

Figure 1.3. Among the fans in attendance for Yankee Stadium's first game was President Warren G. Harding (*right*), seated with dignitaries (April 24, 1923). Library of Congress, George Grantham Bain Collection.

The following year, in 1933, baseball fans had another opportunity to show their favoritism toward Gehrig when they voted him onto the first American League All-Star team. He was named to start at first base on the strength of some 500,000 votes delivered by loyal fans, three times more than future Hall of Famer Jimmie Foxx received. Gehrig went 0 for 2 in the game. Author Robert Greenberger explained the player's election: "Despite not receiving as much press as Ruth, Gehrig had devoted fans around the country," he wrote. "When the [first] all-star game was played in 1933 he was overwhelmingly voted [by fans] to start at first base, beating the Philadelphia Athletics [Hall of Famer] Jimmie Foxx by 185,576 votes."[10]

Years later, in 1939, as Gehrig's skills inexplicably began to wane due to what eventually would be diagnosed as ALS, fans continued to support him. When the Yankees broke spring training, it was clear to everyone that something was terribly wrong with the slugger. Gehrig's hitting was out of whack, so to speak; his fielding was off-kilter, and the big first baseman wasn't moving with the fidelity that was characteristic of Gehrig. Still, when he came to bat on opening day against the Boston Red Sox with two men on base, the fans stood and cheered him loudly, hoping he could turn things around and regain his hitting form of old. As they cheered for Gehrig, he flied out to right field.

Some trace the beginning of indications of Gehrig's ALS as far back as July 13, 1934, when he stumbled and nearly fell while running out a single in Detroit. The incident was later attributed to lumbago, or an unexplained muscle weakness in his back, and there would be more stumbles as the years went by, sometimes accompanied by difficulty breathing. No one considered the problem serious, especially as Gehrig continued to pile up good numbers. In 1934, the year of the first stumble, he hit forty-nine home runs with 166 RBI and batted .363 in an all-star season; in 1937, another all-star season, he hit thirty-seven home runs with 158 RBI and batted .351. Then, his numbers trailed off.

Two months before his speech, on May 2, 1939, when he benched himself permanently, Gehrig received a standing ovation from appreciative Detroit Tigers fans as he sat on the Yankees bench at Briggs Stadium, tears welling up in his eyes. The following month, on June 29, fans in Philadelphia gave him an eight-minute ovation after Athletics manager Connie Mack invited him onto the field before the game. Clearly, fan appreciation of the popular first baseman was indiscriminate of his team affiliation. So popular was Gehrig among teammates and fans, even fans in other cities, that he remained on the team as captain throughout the remainder of the 1939 season. Explained Gehrig in a letter to his wife, "Playing is out of the question."[11]

"He was a special guy," said former Yankee Repoz, considered a future star with the team on a par with Mickey Mantle early in his career. "He epitomized what we all felt once we put on the pinstripes."[12]

Oddly, doctors at the Mayo Clinic, where Gehrig had been undergoing tests, released to the Yankees, who in turn released to the fans, information on his condition on June 19, 1939, the day his diagnosis was confirmed. The fact that they released the information to the public, even before his official retirement announcement was made, is an indicator of his indelible relationship with the fans. They cared about him and wanted the information, and Gehrig and the Yankees understood that.

Just days later, returning home from the renowned medical center in Rochester, Minnesota, Gehrig was greeted at Union Station in Washington, DC, by a group of cheering Boy Scouts on hand to wish him well. Gehrig was touched by the support from the young fans, who were likely oblivious to the fact that he had two years to live.

Through it all, the ups and downs, the home runs, the strikeouts, and even his illness, Gehrig loved his adoring fans. "One thing that helps me more than anything is the letters I receive," he once told the sportswriter Grantland Rice. "They come from every section of the country, from the old and the young. Many of them are marvelous. They prove how many fine people the world has left."[13]

Shortly after Gehrig retired from baseball, one of Gehrig's biggest fans made himself known: New York mayor Fiorello La Guardia. On October 10, 1939, just forty-eight hours after the Yankees' season ended with a World Series sweep of the Cincinnati Reds, La Guardia called Gehrig at his home to offer him an employment opportunity. The New York City Board of Parole had a vacancy, La Guardia said, and, dangling it as a chance for Gehrig to help young men get a fresh start after troubles with the law, he offered the position to New York's newest former ballplayer. The appointment carried a modest $6,000 salary, and it did require a move from the suburbs back into the city.

"I believe you are just the man for the job, and I know you will get a kick out of it," La Guardia told the ailing Gehrig. "It means an opportunity to serve a lot of young fellows who haven't had much of a break from life and could stand a lot of help." Gehrig jumped at the

Figure 1.4. Fans line up at the Yankee Stadium ticket booth in 1923 to, as Lou Gehrig intimated in his farewell speech, express their kindness and encouragement. Library of Congress, George Grantham Bain Collection.

opportunity. "That sounds great," he said, adding, "Thank-you, Mr. Mayor. Thank-you."[14]

Just days removed from baseball, Gehrig already had something, a diversion, perhaps, to occupy his time away from the medical black hole that threatened to envelop him. He owed the opportunity to one of the highest profile fans in New York City: Mayor La Guardia. What's more, the choice of Gehrig to fill the position was brilliant because young men, even those who were down on their luck, admired the former Yankees star. Some of them were true fans of the slugger and could readily benefit from being held accountable by a man they admired.

At about that time, major-league baseball itself became an official fan of Gehrig, temporarily changing its own rules and inducting him into the National Baseball Hall of Fame without the requisite five-year waiting period.

With Gehrig, fandom had no statute of limitation. More than eight decades after Gehrig's death, a Texas fan and longtime physician wrote about one of his favorite players: "Growing up in the 1930s I was an avid baseball fan," Herbert L. Fred wrote. "My favorite team was the New York Yankees, and my favorite players were Babe Ruth, Lou Gehrig, and the great DiMaggio. They all subsequently became prominent members of the Baseball Hall of Fame, but only one of them—Lou Gehrig—became forever linked with medicine."[15] Even in sickness Gehrig's fan base was bolstered.

Another fan, born decades after the slugger died and who never saw him play in a single game, wrote a book about her hero, titled *The Life of Lou Gehrig: Told by a Fan*. "In this unique biography of the man who has inspired so many, Sara Kaden Brunsvold looks at Gehrig from the point of view of a fan, revealing what he and his legacy have been to her and countless other fans," the book description reads.[16]

Through the years, countless books have been written about Gehrig's life. A movie was made, starring Gary Cooper. Articles continue to be written about the man, his career, and the disease that cut it short. Long after his death, Gehrig still resonates with his fans, many of whom, now quite elderly, followed the Yankees as young children when he was blistering drives over the Yankee Stadium right-field wall. Modern players often are counted as fans, too, or at least followers of the Gehrig mystique.

"Everyone who ever joined the Yankees, I'm sure they'd heard of him," said former MVP Shantz, who played for the Yankees from 1957 to 1960. "Gehrig and Ruth and [Tony] Lazzeri and guys like that. I know I'd heard a lot about him."[17]

Certainly, Gehrig was a favorite of fans. In 1999, sixty years after he last swung a bat, Gehrig was named to the Major League Baseball All-Century Team, receiving more votes than any other player. As was fitting, the team was chosen by—who else?—the fans, to whom Gehrig fittingly addressed his "Luckiest Man" speech.

CHAPTER 2

A BAD BREAK

> For the past two weeks you've been reading about a bad break.
>
> —Lou Gehrig, "Luckiest Man" speech

As bad breaks go, Gehrig's was remarkable. It was dreadful. When considering an individual's personal health and the worst-case bad-break scenarios that might occur, Lou Gehrig's disease, officially known as amyotrophic lateral sclerosis, often comes to mind. For starters, it's a neurodegenerative disorder, meaning it renders the nerves useless. It's also progressive, worsening each day that its victim is alive. And, assuming the patient doesn't suffer a heart attack or get hit by a car or die from coronavirus infection in the interim, it usually results in the patient's death. Those unfortunate enough to be diagnosed with ALS can count on one thing: they're probably going to die from it. Almost as bad, patients with ALS often retain their mental clarity, meaning they're fully aware that their health is deteriorating and of how badly their disease will ultimately play out. It's like stumbling to the gallows.

The speed of death varies by patient, and the end is never pleasant. Some patients die slowly, while with others the disease takes relatively little time to run its dastardly course. Stephen Hawking, the renowned British physicist, developed ALS in 1963 at the age of twenty-one and lived another fifty-five years, finally succumbing at the age of seventy-six in 2018. In contrast, the singer Huddie William Ledbetter, aka Lead Belly, went to his grave quickly, dying just months after his diagnosis in 1949.

Most patients aren't as fortunate—or unfortunate—as Hawking, who suffered through an unrelenting deformation despite living more than half a century with ALS. Other famous ALS sufferers have included Academy Award–winning actor David Niven and Cy Young Award–winning pitcher Jim "Catfish" Hunter. Most famous of all is Gehrig, who brought national attention to the then-little-known disease almost overnight and whose name was unambiguously wed to the disorder. The initials *ALS* mean little to most people, but *Lou Gehrig's disease* means everything—it's a physiological horror show.

Making matters worse for Gehrig was his standing as an elite professional baseball player, a man synonymous with strength and good health whose disease was wrapped in a mantle of prosperity. But ALS does not distinguish between those it chastens; it never plays favorites in seeking out victims, and in time Gehrig was just another enfeebled sufferer competing in vain against an incurable disease. More than eighty years later it's still incurable.

ALS was first identified in 1869 by French physician Jean-Martin Charcot, known to many as the father of French neurology; however, it wasn't until Gehrig's high-profile diagnosis seventy years later that the disease began to receive the attention it deserved across the United States and around the world. By terminating the career of one of America's greatest and most highly regarded athletes, a man still in the prime of his career and life, the disease became indelibly intertwined with his name and remains so today. When people develop ALS in the United States, it's usually referred to as Lou Gehrig's disease, although much of the rest of world calls it Charcot's disease.

ALS kills by attacking essential nerve cells in the brain and spinal column. In humans, motor neurons extend from the brain to a person's spinal cord, and from there they reach to muscles from head to toe and from fingertip to fingertip. When motor neurons are rendered lifeless, the brain's ability to initiate and control muscle movement also is neutralized. As voluntary muscle activity is affected during progression of the disease, patients may eventually become paralyzed.

There are two forms of ALS: sporadic and familial. Sporadic ALS, the most common type found in the United States, is identified in up to ninety-five percent of all patients with ALS and may strike anyone at any time, anywhere. Familial ALS, inherited from a family member, is far rarer and accounts for the remainder of all cases identified in the United States, perhaps 5 percent. In those families there's a 50 percent chance that each of the family member's progeny will display the mutated gene, suffering the same fate as Gehrig and ultimately developing ALS with all its thorns.

Although Gehrig's disease was initially confirmed during the 1939 baseball season, there are indications that he first began showing signs of having ALS long before that, perhaps as early as 1934. One incident on the ball field has been examined by baseball experts and sportswriters in hopes of identifying the disease's early appearance in Gehrig. Eighty-eight years later, there is still no consensus.

On July 13 of that year the Yankees faced the Tigers at Briggs Stadium in Detroit. Gehrig, leading off the second inning for the Yankees, drove a single to center field and took off for first base as he normally would. As he ran down the first baseline he inexplicably bent over and nearly fell to the ground as he approached the bag, still managing to reach the base safely with a single. After noticing that his big first baseman appeared to be unable to stand properly, first-base coach Earle Combs called time-out and asked his star what was wrong; third-base coach Art Fletcher was also concerned and joined in the conversation. Gehrig shook off their concern, suggesting that he may have been suffering from the effects of a cold; however, his coaches concluded that Gehrig might have lumbago—a painful lower back disorder. When their on-field conference was over, Gehrig remained in the game, barely reaching second on a single by Ben Chapman and getting doubled up moments later when Bill Dickey lined out to center field. When the inning ended, Gehrig pulled himself out of the ball game.

After Gehrig exited the game, the Yankees trainer worked on his back late into the night; however, the next day it remained bothersome. Wishing to keep his consecutive games streak alive, Gehrig started the contest, singled weakly to right field in his first at bat, trotted laboriously out toward first base, gamely touched the bag, and left the game. The sportswriter James M. Kahn of the *New York Sun*, who covered the Yankees, wrote,

> This was Gehrig's closest escape from having his endurance mark broken, and it is given in detail because it may hold an additional interest for medical men. These attacks occurred occasionally and escaped accurate diagnosis, invariably doubling him over and making it difficult for him to breathe until they wore off in a couple of days. For convenience in reporting them, and because of the absence of anything more definite,

the sportswriters referred to the attacks as lumbago. Gehrig became quite sensitive to the curiosity of the reporters after a while when these attacks hit him, which they did three or four times over a period of four or five years.[1]

As Kahn wrote, from then until he retired, Gehrig suffered similar bouts of lumbago, or cold symptoms, or ALS, or whatever it was that apparently began hampering him on that day in 1934—no one is certain whether that early health scare was idiopathic or a precursor to the disease that would one day take his life. Over the following four years, until his statistics began to trail off during the 1938 season, it didn't really matter to most people what was wrong, and few probably gave it much thought. Except, perhaps, Gehrig and his wife, who likely knew something was chronically amiss.

The seriousness of Gehrig's condition first drew whispers among fellow players and the press corps during the 1938 season, when those close to him noticed hints of a clumsiness they had never seen before in the superstar. He would drop a pen or perhaps stumble while fielding an easy ground ball. McCarthy dropped him to fifth in the batting order, then

Figure 2.1. Joe McCarthy (*left*) joins Washington Nationals manager Bucky Harris to open the 1939 baseball season by raising a flag over the Nationals' home field. Library of Congress, Harris & Ewing Collection.

sixth. Fans in some cities chided him when he came to the plate. Even McCarthy's wife, Elizabeth, jumped into the fray, writing Gehrig a letter of encouragement and noting that the popular slugger was in her prayers.

For a while his hitting improved, and Gehrig was reinstated as the Yankees' cleanup batter. Still, his slumps persisted from time to time—and when he did get a hit there wasn't the same pizzazz in his clout that fans and teammates had come to appreciate. Finally, the home fans began to tease him.

As the season wound down, Gehrig's batting average dipped below the .300 mark and remained there for the first time since 1925, with his run production also suffering. By the end of the season one thing had become apparent to fans, teammates, and the Yankees front office: the Gehrig of 1938 was not the same Gehrig who had dominated the American League over the previous twelve seasons.

Statistics bear that out: in 1937 Gehrig hit .351 with thirty-seven home runs and 159 RBI. The following year, his last one as a full-time player, he hit just .295 with twenty-nine home runs and 114 RBI. There would be just four hits in twenty-eight at bats and zero home runs over the remainder of his ebbing career—the early weeks of the 1939 season, when he averaged a hit every seven at bats. For Gehrig, the genie was about to flee the bottle.

While his statistics for 1938 were subpar for Gehrig, they would have been outstanding for nearly any other player. He had made the American League All-Star team for the seventh time since the game was initiated and finished nineteenth in the balloting for Most Valuable Player. Gehrig wasn't at all satisfied, however, and he began spring training committed to showing those critical of his play that he was still an elite player. Unfortunately, that ship had sailed—at that point Gehrig was struggling to play even average ball.

After the 1938 season, General Manager Barrow had cut Gehrig's salary by $3,000, from $39,000 down to $36,000, a slap in the face by the man who signed him to his original contract and treated him like a son. The move was a prophetic one. Sportswriters were whispering that his career was beginning to wind down, and Gehrig did little to dispel that notion during spring training prior to his final season. His hitting lagged—he batted just .100 during the Yankees' first ten exhibition games, with nothing more than a single to show. Teammates recalled that once during batting practice he swung at nineteen consecutive pitches and missed them all. He also struggled at first base and on two occasions fell down inside the clubhouse. Nonetheless, McCarthy stuck with his once-fearsome first baseman. Perhaps he should have followed his instincts.

Despite Gehrig's slow start and resultant poor production during his final spring training, McCarthy started him at first base on opening day in 1939 and was committed to leaving him in the lineup. After all, Gehrig had owned the position for thirteen years, and McCarthy was going to make sure he played himself out of the lineup rather than bench him prematurely—if at all. Besides, there was the consecutive games streak to consider, one that was still alive at 2,130 games one week into the 1939 season. If Gehrig reversed his trajectory and continued on to perform like the Gehrig of old, so much the better. The streak would be preserved, and no lineup change would be necessary; however, that wouldn't happen—not with ALS.

"When you start playing the game as a professional, you're out there every day, grinding day in and day out, long bus rides, twilight-night doubleheaders, playing ten, twelve, fifteen, even twenty days or more without a day off," said former Yankee Andy McGaffigan, who played for the team during his rookie season in 1981. "It made me think, 'Well, dadgum, Gehrig did that for fourteen years in a row!'"[2]

Gehrig started in the Yankees' first eight regular-season games in 1939, and he played miserably. In twenty-eight at bats, he managed no extra-base hits and drove in only one run. He made two errors in the field, putting him on a trajectory to make a whopping thirty-nine miscues over the course of a 154-game season. In sixteen previous campaigns Gehrig had never committed more than eighteen errors in a single season (that low point occurred twice, in 1928 and 1932), and anything approaching forty would have been disastrous for the aging star. So would a season with few home runs, few extra-base hits, few RBI, few runs scored, and a low batting average. Something had to give.

On Tuesday, May 2, a week into the 1939 season, Gehrig was hitting less than half his lifetime batting average of .340. Discouraged by his early poor play, he quietly visited McCarthy in his Detroit hotel room and asked to be removed immediately from the Yankees' starting lineup. The request, which would end the slugger's consecutive games streak, had been two days in coming (see table A.1 in the appendix for statistics from Gehrig's final game).

"I decided last Sunday night on this move," he said. "I haven't been a bit of good to the team since the season started. It would not be fair to the boys, to Joe [McCarthy], or to the baseball public for me to try going on."[3] Reluctantly, his manager complied. The streak was over and so, too, was Gehrig's career. He would never play again.

While Gehrig remained with the team as captain, initially delivering the lineup card to home plate before each game, standing near the infield as the Yankee players loosened up, and sitting with his teammates on the bench during games, his focus would soon shift to what he eventually would describe in his famous speech as "*a bad break*"—his affliction with amyotrophic lateral sclerosis. Eleanor contacted the Mayo Clinic, where a medical team led by Charles Mayo, son of the medical center's esteemed cofounder, evaluated Gehrig over a one-week period. Physicians concluded that their high-profile patient was suffering from ALS, exhibiting the early stages of a methodical and debilitating nerve and muscle breakdown. During the three years that doctors predicted he might live—he would only live two—Gehrig would eventually suffer progressive paralysis, and his heart and lungs would stop functioning altogether. The man who many thought would play and live forever would experience a slow, painful, and difficult death.

Gehrig had only two months to digest the Mayo Clinic's medical findings before the Yankees announced they would honor him with Lou Gehrig Appreciation Day. In two short months he had gone from American League All-Star and Yankees superstar to baseball retiree and a man suffering with, in his words, a deadly bad break, one that might have made it challenging for him to complete at even the Little League level. The bad break, which broke the Yankees' spirit, also broke the hearts of fans who for more than a decade had cheered Gehrig on as a team leader and seemingly indestructible force. As spring turned into summer and Gehrig disappeared from the baseball limelight into a netherworld of doctor appointments and physical compromise, one thing was clear: for baseball's Iron Horse, the barn door was closed tight. The worst was yet to come.

CHAPTER 3

LUCKIEST MAN

Today I consider myself the luckiest man on the face of the earth.

—Lou Gehrig, "Luckiest Man" speech

As the sporty man in dark slacks strode toward the microphone, the scene at Yankee Stadium was eerily reminiscent of Gehrig's farewell appearance three decades earlier. Mickey Mantle, one of the all-time great Yankees, was saying goodbye on Mickey Mantle Day, June 8, 1969, twenty-nine years and eleven months after Lou Gehrig Appreciation Day and held, appropriately, at the same venue. Mantle was presented that day by former teammate Joe DiMaggio, who had played alongside Gehrig toward the end of the Iron Horse's career and was on hand when he retired in similar fashion; he proudly introduced his friend by offering him a plaque commemorating his years as a beloved Yankee, to be hung near DiMaggio's own marker in center field at Yankee Stadium. Just as Gehrig's uniform number four and DiMaggio's number five had been duly retired, so was Mantle's number seven pulled from the rack on that sentimental New York afternoon, never to be worn by anyone again.

"Gehrig's influence on the Yankees was certainly obvious by the memorials [to him and other Yankee greats] out in center field," former Yankee Andy McGaffigan said. "We walked right by them when we went out to the bullpen."[1]

On his special day, Yankee greats from Mantle's era were introduced in much the same way that Gehrig's teammates were paraded onto the field in 1939. During his storied eighteen-year career, Mantle had faced his own kind of adversity, including numerous injuries that often kept him out of the Yankees lineup and a serious drinking problem that likely claimed his life—he died of alcohol-related cancer in 1995,[2] at the youthful age of sixty-three. With those self-inflicted hardships in hand, Mantle had the keen insight and wherewithal to acknowledge Gehrig with a note of understanding that only men of similar status could share. "I've often wondered how a man who knew he was gonna die could stand here and say that he was the *luckiest man* in the world," Mantle said. "But now I think I know how Lou Gehrig felt."[3]

Mantle's comment notwithstanding, the greatest ponderable emanating from Gehrig's "Luckiest Man" speech is how someone who had just lost his ability to earn a living, shed the adulation of fans around the country, and departed from the camaraderie of his many Yankee teammates, someone who was then in a fight for his life against a dreaded disease that few people were familiar with and that had no cure, could somehow declare himself "*the luckiest man on the face of the earth.*" Lucky in what respect, many must have wondered.

Figure 3.1. Lou Gehrig in 1924, the year before he joined the Yankees. *New York Daily News.*

"I believe he was really self-aware of his position in life," McGaffigan said. "Humble, unassuming. He was probably a great teammate."[4]

Luck, it seems, is in the beholder's eye. Maturity, on the other hand, is proactive: it's the ability to look at the big picture from birth to impending death and offer an evaluation such as Gehrig's determination that his so-called luck had been largely good and, for at least the moment, remained so despite appearances to the contrary, in his case a fatal disease. Despite the fight he was just beginning to wage, one nearly as epic as his famous speech, Gehrig concluded his luck had been—and still remained—largely good.

It is hard to imagine the extent of what Gehrig deep down must have perceived as incredibly bad luck. Being squeezed from his grip at that moment were a number of other essentials in his once-happy life: the people he loved the most, including his wife, Eleanor, to whom he'd been married for only a handful of apparently blissful years; his parents, who had labored to teach him right from wrong, given him the moral compass that people who knew him most admired, raised him to work hard and achieve success, and whom he had lived with for thirty of his thirty-six years; and many close friends and teammates, including the Yankees catcher Bill Dickey, his neighbor and longtime sportswriter and columnist John Kieran, and his manager McCarthy, who considered Gehrig the son he never had and whom Gehrig in turn probably considered the type of father he wished he'd had. To many observers, the slugger was far from lucky at that moment in his intractable life. In fact, he was downright cursed. Still, he trudged on with his burden until the very end, which in fact came quickly.

Turn it around, and each of those points may be blessings in disguise; in Gehrig's eyes they represented the good luck he would speak of in his speech. He had been blessed with two great parents who dearly loved him; a wife who loved, admired, and protected him; and one of the finest managers who ever donned a baseball uniform and a genuinely wonderful human being. In that regard he may truly have been *the luckiest man on the face of the earth*. Luckier than many, anyway.

In the Selznick wartime movie *Since You Went Away*, flier Johnny Mahoney, son of the town grocer, reconnects with a family friend played by actress Claudette Colbert at a canteen dance held in a darkened hanger. Moments before departing on a flight exercise, the young man expresses to Colbert how fortunate he has been his entire life and how he expects to survive the war through that very same kind of luck. He then departs the dance with a broad smile on his face and a skip in his step, only to have his plane crash in a fireball just outside of town, killing the exuberantly optimistic flier upon impact. So it goes with good luck.

Gehrig's life had been similar, full of good fortune from the beginning to then. However, in mid-1939, when his ALS diagnosis was first revealed to the admiring public, Gehrig's plane was spiraling downward. The main difference between him and the cinematic Mahoney was that Gehrig knew his once-carefree life was crashing around him and he still considered himself a lucky man. Lucky or unlucky? At the very least it was inexplicable, at least to Gehrig.

"I just can't understand," Gehrig said before his diagnosis. "I am not sick. The stomach complaint which was revealed last year in three separate examinations I underwent has been cleared up by observance of a strict diet. My eye is sharp, yet I was not swinging as of old. I reduced the weight of my bat from thirty-six to thirty-three ounces, thinking a change might work to my advantage, but it didn't. I went back to the thirty-six and it was the same."[5]

Therein lay the paradox.

"His greatest record doesn't show in the book," Kieran wrote. "It was the absolute reliability of Henry Louis Gehrig. He could be counted upon. He was there every day at the ballpark, bending his back and ready to break his neck to win for his side. He was there day after day and year after year. He never sulked or whined or went into a pot or a huff. He was the answer to a manager's dream."[6] He was, until he wasn't. In 1939 the dream became a nightmare.

For much of his short life Gehrig truly had been an unlucky man. He was raised in relative poverty and teased about his German heritage, which earned him the nickname "Heinie," an obvious disparagement. His father had difficulty supporting the family. His mother was overbearing. He suffered with chronic shyness to the point that he tried out for the high school baseball team only as a last resort. He faced permanent expulsion from the Columbia University athletics program, including the baseball and football teams, for foolishly using an alias to even more foolishly compete for a minor-league team that probably recompensed him with next to nothing. His impromptu tryout with the fabled New York Giants was a bust in the eyes of famed manager John McGraw, made worse by the fact that Gehrig performed amazingly well on short notice, was still treated rudely, and probably deserved strong consideration for a professional contract rather than the discouragement he suffered at the hands of the legendary skipper. As a result, Gehrig's baseball career nearly fizzled before it dazzled.

Then, his luck changed emphatically and seemingly forever. Yankees scout Paul Krichell inadvertently saw Gehrig play, and the following day he convinced Ed Barrow, the Yankees general manager, to sign the young man to a contract. Barrow, hesitant at first, finally agreed.

"I did not go there to look at Lou Gehrig," Krichell said many years later. "I did not even know what position he played, but he played in the outfield against Rutgers College and socked a couple of balls a

Figure 3.2. Paul Krichell, the Yankees scout who discovered Lou Gehrig, in 1911. Library of Congress, George Grantham Bain Collection.

mile. I sat up and took notice. I saw a tremendous youth, with powerful arms and terrific legs. I said, 'Here is a kid who can't miss.'"[7]

From there it was seemingly all downhill for Gehrig, at least in the luck department. In 1925, with Yankees first baseman Wally Pipp slumping and reportedly ill—according to lore, he was suffering with a headache—Gehrig replaced him in the lineup and remained the team's first sacker for the next thirteen seasons. He won two American League Most Valuable Player Awards. He hit four home runs in a single game. He hit three home runs in a game three other times. He twice hit for the cycle. He hit nearly five hundred lifetime home runs, the gold standard for greatness. He won a batting title. He was an All-Star in each of the seven seasons he competed in once the game was introduced. He won three home-run titles. At one time or another he led the league in runs scored, doubles, triples, and RBI. He recorded two hundred or more hits in a season eight times.

"We had a quip that when somebody took a day off, and this was true no matter what [baseball] organization I was with, he would jokingly be called Wally Pipp," the one-time Yankee McGaffigan said, adding that the Yankees of his own era had a culture of excellence that the then owner George Steinbrenner demanded.[8] Certainly Gehrig, without even trying, turned Pipp into a household name. Fred Kipp, who in 1960 spent a month playing for the Yankees at the tail end of his short major-league career, offered a similar assessment: "In the minor leagues, if someone got hurt and was out for four or five days, players would ask, 'Who is that—Pipp? You better get back in there or someone is going to take your job.'"[9]

After building momentum over sixteen seasons with the Yankees and creating a comfortable life for himself and his wife, the roof fell in on Gehrig in 1939, his seventeenth season. His string of luck came to a crashing halt. Lou Gehrig was no longer lucky.

Or was he?

"*For the past two weeks you've been reading about a bad break*," he told fans at the packed Yankee Stadium on the day that he retired, getting right to the point. "*Today I consider myself the luckiest man on the face of the earth*." One bad break doesn't make a lifetime, he must have reasoned.

At the moment he spoke those words, Gehrig didn't appear to be the luckiest man or even lucky at all. He stared nervously down, scraped his cleats at the dirt, and appeared to be trying to reconcile if not adjust to and accept his unpropitious fate. The luck that he spoke of was nowhere to be seen then, least of all on the faces of his teammates, those in the press box, and those of people in the crowd, many of whom were teary-eyed over his fate. There were plenty of tears to go around, and doubtless no one in the stadium considered Gehrig a lucky man at that moment. Except for one person, perhaps: Gehrig himself.

He may have been lucky, at that. That day he likely returned from the stadium to a comfortable and safe home, knowing he had earned that comfort with the fruits of a great career that had suddenly come to the close that he knew it one day must. Accompanied by his loving wife, he was probably met at the door by his faithful dog, Afra. For a while he and Eleanor continued to host close friends at their home, probably for quiet dinners and conversation. He fished with friends as his health permitted. His parents visited. He even had a mother-in-law who treated him like a son. Those without such blessings might argue that the things he was still able to enjoy made him *the luckiest man on the face of the earth.*

Just weeks earlier, his luck was in doubt as Gehrig had received a death sentence, revealed in a letter from Mayo Clinic doctor Harold C. Habein that was released to reporters by the Yankees organization. Addressed "to whom it may concern," it read,

> This is to certify that Mr. Lou Gehrig has been under examination at the Mayo Clinic from June 13 to June 19, 1939, inclusive.
>
> After a careful and complete examination, it was found that he is suffering from amyotrophic lateral sclerosis. This type of illness involves the motor pathways and cells of the central nervous system and in lay terms is known as a form of chronic poliomyelitis [infantile paralysis].
>
> The nature of this trouble makes it such that Mr. Gehrig will be unable to continue his active participation as a baseball player inasmuch as it is advisable that he conserve his muscular energy. He could, however, continue in some executive capacity.[10]

Lucky? It appeared not. Then came The Speech, where the once-reticent Gehrig surprised everyone by boldly speaking to a packed audience. It was the same confidence he had shown on the field.

"I saw strong men weep this afternoon, expressionless umpires swallow hard and emotion pump the hearts and glaze the eyes of 60,000 baseball fans at Yankee Stadium," wrote the *Washington Post*'s Shirley Povich, who scribed for the newspaper from 1923 until his death in 1998—three quarters of a century.[11]

Under similar circumstances, most would have difficulty expressing the private thoughts that Gehrig did to even a handful of close friends—let alone 62,000 people, most of whom he had never met. Not Gehrig. "That's pretty special," said Rick Dempsey, who played with the Yankees from 1973 to 1976. "It was probably as memorable as any game-winning hit or home run that ever was. The courage it must have taken for him to say that, knowing he had a disease that he wasn't going to survive. What a person he was—I idolized everything about him."[12]

While little resembling luck bubbled up for Gehrig that day or, it seemed, for anyone else at the ballpark—with the exception of his replacement, Babe Dahlgren, who went four for seven in the two games—luck sometimes comes in a black box. At last, the pressure was off for Gehrig to perform day in and day out in front of large, scrutinizing crowds. He could finally relax at home. After he died, Gehrig was hoisted to legend status. Major-league baseball whisked him into the Hall of Fame. His speech was elevated to consideration as one for the ages. People admired him, perhaps more so than when he was swatting balls to all corners of Yankee Stadium and often over the right-field fence. Politicians offered him employment.

Considering the entire package—Gehrig's life, his career, the superb achievements he left behind for the baseball world to contemplate, and most of all his remarkable speech—it is useful to ponder whether with our own lives still intact, our families around to embrace us, our jobs and careers secure, and the many other blessings most of us are able to enjoy, perhaps in contrast we, as fans and admirers, are really the lucky ones. It took Gehrig's difficult, lingering illness to put that in perspective, and he may have sensed that scenario was his broader purpose beyond baseball: to inspire others. If even in facing death he foresaw that possibility, that those hearing him talk for the last time would be encouraged and enriched by the optimism in his "Luckiest Man" speech, then at that moment Gehrig truly may have been *the luckiest man on the face of the earth.*

CHAPTER 4

MEN IN UNIFORM

> When you look around, wouldn't you consider it a privilege to associate yourself with such fine-looking men as are standing in uniform in this ballpark today?
>
> —Lou Gehrig, "Luckiest Man" speech

As men *standing in uniform* watched attentively from the Yankee Stadium infield, a robust gentleman dressed in a light summer suit with an open collar strode past everyone and up to the waiting microphones.

The smiling, easygoing man hadn't swung a bat in four years, but somehow he looked as though at any moment he could send a ball streaking skyward over the right-field fence for one of his signature home runs. Throw some pinstripes on his corpulent frame, and the man with the dark stockings covering his spindly legs was probably good to go.

On Lou Gehrig Appreciation Day, it was more than appropriate that the one-time face of the New York Yankees, the indomitable Babe Ruth, deliver a short introduction. What the Babe said that day fit nicely with the manner in which Gehrig would moments later describe his beloved former teammates, some of them members of the famed Murderers' Row of 1927, and many of them long retired from the game of baseball.

"In 1927, Lou was with us, and I say that was the greatest ball club the Yankees ever had," Ruth said.[1] Indeed, by most accounts it was. The 1927 Yankees won 110 games and lost forty-four for a winning percentage of .714, eighth best in baseball history and fifth best at that time. They won the American League pennant by nineteen games over the second-place Philadelphia Athletics and fifty-nine games over the last-place Boston Red Sox. In the World Series that year, the Yankees swept the Pittsburgh Pirates in four games, outscoring the Bucs 23–10. Ruth slugged the only two home runs that the Yankees would collect and batted a sterling .400 in the Series, while Gehrig hit .308 with two doubles and two triples—all of his hits went for extra bases. Wilcy Moore, an unheralded rookie right-hander who posted his best record in 1927 with nineteen wins and a 2.28 ERA, won two games for the Yankees and recorded a 0.84 ERA to lead a pitching staff that included luminaries like Hall of Famers Waite Hoyt and Herb Pennock.

"The 1927 New York Yankees are the standard by which all baseball teams are measured, even by those that have eclipsed some of the club's achievements," wrote Christine Daniels in the *Los Angeles Times*. "The '27 Yankees made their mark with offensive exploits that seemed otherworldly at the time, their reputation driven by two of the game's most legendary larger-than-life figures, Babe Ruth and Lou Gehrig."[2]

In addition to Ruth, who had left the Yankees to once again join the Red Sox after what for him had been a mediocre 1934 season, notable former teammates who attended the pregame ceremonies that day included Joe Dugan, Hoyt, Mark Koenig, Tony Lazzeri, and Bob Meusel, all of them starters in game one of the 1927 World Series; Benny Bengough, a starter in game two; Pennock, a starter in game three; the venerable Pipp, a member of the original Murderers' Row of 1918 and a man who had figured prominently in Gehrig's ascension to regular first baseman for the Yankees; Earle Combs; Wally Schang; George Pipgras (an umpire that day); Everett Scott; and Bob Shawkey, who retired after the 1927 season. Gehrig, Ruth, Koenig, Lazzeri, and Meusel were all members of a later version of Murderers' Row in 1927. Perhaps best known, aside from Gehrig and Ruth, were Lazzeri, Hoyt, and Pennock.

Acquired by the Yankees in 1925, Lazzeri went on to become perhaps the finest second baseman in Yankees history. That's quite an achievement considering that Lazzeri, who was disenchanted over frequent assignments with various minor-league teams, quit the game at the youthful age of nineteen. However, by 1926 he was back in action for good, this time with the big club, slugging eighteen home runs and driving in 117 runners during his rookie season.

His elevation to the big-league Yankees was not unexpected. During the 1925 season, playing for Salt Lake City of the Pacific Coast League, Lazzeri had hit sixty home runs, driven in 222 runners, scored 202 runs,

Figure 4.1. Bob Meusel (*right*), a member of the Yankees' feared Murderers' Row, chats with brother Emil "Irish" Meusel of the New York Giants, 1923. Library of Congress, George Grantham Bain Collection.

and batted .355. Not even the Babe put up such significant RBI and runs-scored numbers. Over fourteen seasons with the Yankees, Cubs, Dodgers, and Giants, Lazzeri, who hit 191 minor-league home runs, batted .292 with 1,840 hits, 178 homers, and 1,194 RBI. He was inducted into the Baseball Hall of Fame in 1991.

"Around New York I used to hear that expression, 'Once a Dodger, always a Dodger,'" Lazzeri once said. "But how about, 'Once a Yankee, always a Yankee?' There never was anything better than that. You never get over it."[3]

The Hall of Famer Pennock was sold to the Yankees in 1923, the year Yankee Stadium opened, after stints with the Philadelphia Athletics, with whom he debuted at age eighteen, and the Boston Red Sox. Eventually rising to become the ace of the Athletics' pitching staff, he was traded to Boston halfway through the 1915 season following conflicts with the manager, Connie Mack.

It was with the Yankees that Pennock really ascended. In eleven seasons, from 1923 to 1934, he won 159 games and lost ninety, winning twenty-three contests in 1926. Over twenty-two seasons, his record was 241–162, and he boasted a 3.60 lifetime ERA. He was inducted into the Hall of Fame in 1948, the year he died following a stroke.

Hoyt, a native of Brooklyn, signed a contract with the New York Giants at the age of fifteen, then spent the next two seasons playing in the minor leagues. As a rookie pitcher he played in only one game for the Giants, in 1916, then was dealt to the Red Sox and eventually the Yankees in 1921, where he spent the next ten seasons perfecting his game. While pitching for the Yankees, Hoyt excelled, notching 154 of his 237 career wins, including twenty-two in 1927 and twenty-three in 1928. By the time the 1927 season rolled around, Hoyt was considered the staff ace on the greatest team ever.

After retiring from baseball in 1938, Hoyt spent twenty-four years as a baseball broadcaster. He achieved what must have been a record for baseball announcers when he spoke about Ruth on the air for two hours after the Babe's death from cancer was announced in 1948. In 1969, three decades after his retirement, Hoyt was voted into the National Baseball Hall of Fame by the organization's Veterans Committee.

The other old-timers in attendance that day—Dugan (he hit .269 for the 1927 Yankees), Koenig (.285), Bengough (.281), Pipp (.260), Schang (.318), Scott (he retired before the 1927 season), and Shawkey (2–3 with a 2.89 ERA; his final season was 1927)—were journeyman ballplayers

Figure 4.2. Bob Shawkey warms up with the Philadelphia Athletics in 1914, one year before joining the Yankees. He retired after the team's legendary 1927 season. Library of Congress, George Grantham Bain Collection.

who obviously cared enough about Gehrig to be on hand for his farewell, some of them even flying in from out of state. Added to the mix were Gehrig's current teammates, a roster of players that included Lefty Gomez, Red Ruffing, his best friend Dickey, Frank Crosetti, Gehrig's replacement

Dahlgren, Red Rolfe, Tommy Henrich, George Selkirk, and, of course, future legend DiMaggio—a rookie in 1936 and the second-highest-paid player on the 1939 team. Who earned the most money? Gehrig.

Gomez. Ruffing. Dickey. Crosetti. Dahlgren. Rolfe. Henrich. Selkirk. DiMaggio. These were the players whom Gehrig considered it "*a privilege to associate . . . with*," as he declared in his speech. Judging by the legion of players, the *men . . . in uniform*, who paid tribute to the big first baseman on his special day, the feeling among them was mutual. In their minds, there would never be another Lou Gehrig.

CHAPTER 5

AN HONOR

> Sure, I'm lucky. Who wouldn't consider it an honor to have known Jacob Ruppert?
>
> —Lou Gehrig, "Luckiest Man" speech

Over the past century, one name more than any other has come to symbolize the New York Yankees baseball organization: Babe Ruth. There should be two.

If Ruth was, as former Yankee Reggie Jackson once purportedly described himself, the straw that stirred the drink, then Ruppert purchased that straw, manufactured the drink that became the Yankees, and established the brasserie that was Yankee Stadium. Perhaps no person in the history of that organization has made more significant contributions to the most successful franchise in major-league history than the gentlemanly Ruppert.

It was Ruppert, along with his business partner, Tillinghast L'Hommedieu "Cap" Huston, who purchased the Yankees in 1915 for an eye-popping $450,000. At that time, the team owned no ballpark, possessed minimal prestige, and fielded few truly outstanding players. Three years later, in 1918, Ruppert hired Miller Huggins as manager, and things began to change. A year later, he transacted one of the great acquisitions in baseball history, purchasing Ruth from the Red Sox for a mere $25,000—chump change, as it turned out. The pitcher/slugger had hit .322 with twenty-nine home runs and 113 RBI during his final year with the Red Sox; however, once he arrived in New York his stock began to soar, and his numbers jumped to .376 with fifty-four home runs and 135 RBI during his first season in Yankees pinstripes. He would pitch only five more innings during the rest of his career.

Four years later, in 1923, Ruppert finally gave the team the home it had longed for, using more than two million dollars of his own money to build Yankee Stadium in the Bronx. When he signed Lou Gehrig later that same year, the Yankees suddenly had a cadre of bona fide present and future stars, including Ruth, Bob Meusel (a future member of the team's famed Murderers' Row), and Waite Hoyt.

The newcomer Gehrig, who within three short years would become a mainstay in his own right and a future Hall of Famer himself, would have to wait his turn for stardom to come his way. For the Yankees, the wait was well worth it.

Figure 5.1. Jacob Ruppert at Yankee Stadium. Library of Congress, George Grantham Bain Collection.

"I always had good impression of Lou Gehrig," said Bill Virdon, National League Rookie of the Year in 1955 and manager of the Yankees from 1974 to 1975. "He was a player who could do everything. He always gave it all he had, and [as a manager] I thought that was the way to play."[1]

It was the scout Paul Krichell, a former catcher for the St. Louis Browns who was then working under Ruppert as the head of the Yankees' scouting system, who convinced Gehrig to sign with the team after watching him single-handedly destroy Rutgers on the baseball diamond. "I'd want that guy in my lineup in every game," Krichell told Columbia coach Andy Coakley, who had played in the big leagues for three teams from 1902 to 1909. Calling Yankees general manager Ed Barrow on the telephone, Krichell told him, "I think I've found another Babe Ruth."[2] He had indeed, and Krichell, after meeting with Gehrig and encouraging him to talk things over with his coach, brought him to Barrow at 10:00 a.m. the next day. Barrow, whom owner Ruppert leaned heavily on for all player personnel moves, immediately signed the young man to a $2,400 contract that allowed him to finish his season with Columbia before reporting to the Yankees for the remainder of the 1923 season.

Signing Gehrig paid dividends to the Yankees for the next seventeen seasons, just as Ruppert's hand had brought success to the Yankees for eight years prior to that. From 1915 through Ruppert's death six months before Gehrig's "Luckiest Man" speech, the Yankees won the American League pennant ten times and turned seven of those pennants into World Series titles, eight if you count the 1939 world championship that occurred shortly after Ruppert's death.

Jacob Ruppert Jr. was born on August 5, 1867, at his family's mansion on Ninety-Third Street and Fifth Avenue in New York City, the son of a wealthy brewery owner. As a boy he attended Columbia Grammar School, where he played baseball to no apparent acclaim, and he later applied for admission to the School of Mines at Columbia University but never enrolled; neither did he follow through on a coveted appointment to West Point. Instead, his autocratic father had other ideas, and Jacob Jr. began working at Jacob Ruppert Brewery while still in his teens. His schooling was at that point completed. "I forgot about college and about West Point and proceeded to become a brewer," he said.[3]

Ruppert began working at the brewery as a common laborer when he was eighteen, and by the age of twenty he had graduated from the low-level drudgery of that assignment to the business department, which he preferred to manual labor for obvious reasons. In 1891 Ruppert, then

Figure 5.2. Andy Coakley, Gehrig's coach at Columbia University, ca. 1910. Library of Congress, George Grantham Bain Collection.

twenty-three, was named general manager of the brewery by his aging father, and the brewery soon grew to become one of the largest in the entire country. Perhaps reflecting that swift success, Ruppert eventually became chairman of the board and president of the United States Brewers' Association. Ruppert enjoyed two high-profile stop-offs along the way, however. In 1886, while working at the brewery, he joined the Seventh Regiment of the New York National Guard and three years later was named a colonel. Thereafter, and for the rest of his life, he would affectionately be known as Colonel Ruppert.

In 1898, at the still-young age of thirty-one, Ruppert was elected to the first of four terms as a member of Congress, representing the fifteenth congressional district in New York City as a Democrat. He was re-elected in 1900, 1902 (from the sixteenth congressional district), and 1904 before retiring from Congress in 1906.

During his tenure in the House of Representatives, Ruppert performed without apparent distinction, although he served as a member of the Committee on the Militia and the Committee on Immigration and Naturalization. News reports at the time described him as extremely modest and someone who never made a speech on the House floor, although he served with dignity and rarely failed to complete his duties. Those same qualities would be displayed in widescreen during the twenty-four years that Ruppert owned the Yankees.

While his congressional experience may have been unspectacular, Ruppert's private life was something else. In 1912 he engaged in a road race against a wealthy garage owner; the colonel rode a motorcycle, and the mechanic drove an automobile. The race concluded when the man's car broadsided a tree, killing him.

When his father died in 1915, Ruppert inherited Jacob Ruppert Brewery. It was later that year when William Devery and Frank Farrell, original owners of the Yankees, decided to sell the ball club. With his plate rapidly filling with responsibilities, Ruppert, who never married, nonetheless joined Cap Huston as the duo jumped at the opportunity to become owners of the New York Yankees, named as such in 1913 when the nickname "Highlanders" was dropped. Ruppert said many years later that his boyhood ambition had been to play in the major leagues. Failing that, he achieved what he believed was the next best thing: ownership of a major-league franchise.

In 1921 the Yankees won their first American League pennant, under Ruppert as owner and his manager Huggins. In fact, the Yankees would win three pennants in a row, from 1921 to 1923, and their first world championship was under Ruppert's ownership in 1923—the same year Yankee Stadium was built.

There would be three more pennants in succession from 1926 to 1928 and two world championships during that three-year span—in 1927 and 1928. At last, the Yankees were on a roll that never really stopped until 1965 when the club began a string of eleven consecutive seasons without winning a pennant. Under Ruppert's ownership there never was a dearth of pennants or World Series titles—the Yankees won the series

52 | Bronx Epitaph

Figure 5.3. Jacob Ruppert (*right*) with baseball commissioner Kenesaw Mountain Landis and an unidentified boy. Library of Congress, George Grantham Bain Collection.

in 1923, 1927, 1928, 1932, 1936, 1937, and 1938. They also won in1939, nine months after Ruppert's death.

Mutually respectful relationships can be accurately analyzed through the lens of significant financial negotiations, and Gehrig's bond with Ruppert is no exception. A contract discussion following the Yankees' 1927 world championship season underscored the mutual respect that both men had for each other. Gehrig was coming off one of the best seasons he would have as a player: he had won the first of his two Most Valuable Player awards, batting .373, slugging forty-seven home runs, and leading the league with 173 RBI. As their coveted cleanup hitter, he had helped lead the Yankees to a World Series title, hitting .308 with a pair of doubles and triples. If the All-Star Game had been in play at that time, Gehrig certainly would have made the American League squad.

With those impressive offensive numbers to his credit and a world championship in tow, Gehrig, one of the most consequential hitters for a ball club considered among the best ever assembled, believed he was due a salary increase. However, shy as he was and reluctant to cause even ripples in the front office, Gehrig was hesitant to ask Ruppert for more money. Finally, he acquiesced to his own sensibilities.

Having been through the salary wars himself, Ruth offered his teammate, who finally decided he would seek more money, some practical advice on how best to approach Ruppert, an astute businessman who knew a player's worth and could hold his ground in salary negotiations. "Don't accept the first contract that Ruppert offers," Ruth told his teammate. "No matter what offer he puts on the table, insist on $10,000 more. When the negotiations are over, make sure you don't settle for a penny less than $30,000."[4]

Gehrig heeded his teammate's advice and visited Ruppert at the brewery, hoping for a quick settlement. While the amount of money that Gehrig requested was never revealed, Ruppert liked and respected his gentlemanly first baseman, and the two quickly settled on a multiyear contract for $25,000 annually. Even though the figure was slightly low in Ruth's estimation, Ruppert maintained his respect for Gehrig, everyone was happy with the deal, and the three-year contract marked a substantial raise for the first baseman—although well below what the Bambino was earning. Gehrig's value to the club was palpable, and not just in terms of his ability to pound a baseball. "He was a man who everyone looked up to and respected," former Yankees manager Bill Virdon said of Gehrig. "He set a good example, and everyone wanted to be like him."[5]

The raise paid off, as Gehrig helped his team to a four-game sweep of the St. Louis Cardinals in the 1928 World Series, hitting a blistering .545 with four home runs and nine RBI. It was after the series that Ruth and Gehrig performed some hijinks on Ruppert that underscored their congenial relationship with the Yankees boss. Other owners might not have been so accepting of such an invasive prank, but given the circumstances Ruppert took the prank in stride.

Returning to New York by train, the two stars broke into Ruppert's stateroom, where he and a friend, Colonel Fred Wattenberg, were enjoying some much-deserved rest. While the perennially rowdy Ruth emerged from the stateroom waving Ruppert's pajama shirt like a flag, Gehrig retrieved a piece of Wattenberg's sleeping attire. Ruppert, understandably appreciative of the duo's outstanding performances in the series—Ruth had hit .625 with three home runs and four RBI of his own—did not penalize either man for his sophomoric behavior, each of whom he genuinely liked.

Although Ruppert, ever the businessman, understood the significant worth of his hard-hitting first baseman, he held fast to Gehrig through frenzied calls to break up the Yankees as the 1929 season approached and the team eyed its third consecutive world championship. Ruppert could have sold or traded Gehrig for a vast profit of either money or players, but he steadfastly maintained his allegiance to the slugger. If Ruth was the soul of the Yankees, then Gehrig was its heart—and Ruppert wanted him around. He would never consider selling Gehrig, not for any price.

"I have no intention of selling Gehrig or any of my players who, in the judgment of Miller Huggins, can help the team to win another pennant, if possible, in 1929," Ruppert said in a prepared statement. "I not only have no thoughts of breaking up the Yankees, but Ed Barrow, Huggins, and myself will exert our best efforts to strengthen them."[6]

In 1932 it was Ruth's turn to barter with Ruppert over a new contract, and the colonel used Gehrig's success on the field to undercut the Babe by pointing out that Ruth was not the only player bringing fans into the stadium. "I suppose Gehrig didn't help draw all those big crowds last summer," he said sarcastically.[7] He also cut Gehrig's salary from $25,000 down to $23,000 despite his forty-six home runs and career-high 185 RBI the previous season.

By 1933, after addressing his prize slugger as Mr. Gehrig for the past decade, Ruppert began calling him Louis, a salutation that expressed his obvious endearment. After Gehrig played in his 1,308th consecutive game to break the major-league record, the Yankees owner sent him a telegram expressing his heartfelt appreciation for a fine and long-standing effort. Wrote Ruppert, "Accept my heartiest congratulations upon the splendid record of continuous service and accomplishment which you have just completed. My best wishes are with you for many additional years of success."[8] Five years later, Ruppert again expressed pride in his slugger upon the 1938 premiere of the movie *Rawhide*, starring Gehrig and a host of no-name actors. Gehrig had at last found a way to earn some extra money, and Ruppert was pleased,[9] not only for "Louis" but for his lovely wife, Eleanor.

That same year, as his streak hit 1,999 games, Eleanor urged her husband to skip the 2,000th game, believing he needed relief from the pressure and that 1,999 consecutive games would be easier for people to remember. Gehrig, a consummate company man, didn't see it that way and was fearful of hurting the colonel, who had orchestrated a special ceremony at Yankee Stadium. "He'd never forgive me if I didn't show up," Gehrig said.[10]

Gehrig did show up, receiving from his boss a large, sweet-smelling, horseshoe-shaped floral arrangement, which he draped around his neck and wore home like Man o' War—Ruppert was pleased to have Gehrig on hand if for no other reason than for him to receive the gift.[11] Also present were a host of photographers, who recorded Gehrig's achievement that day with plenty of pictures. The event itself and Ruppert's generosity and other kindnesses meant a lot to Gehrig, and he never forgot them—as was apparent when he told the restive crowd it was "*an honor to have known Jacob Ruppert*."

CHAPTER 6

EMPIRE BUILDER

> Also, the builder of baseball's greatest empire, Ed Barrow?
>
> —Lou Gehrig, "Luckiest Man" speech

From the earliest moments of Lou Gehrig's great career, Yankees executive Ed Barrow had an impact. Their relationship began on April 26, 1923, when the scout Paul Krichell, a Barrow hire, recommended him to the team business manager Barrow as a likely future Yankees star. The assessment must have sounded convincing; within days the Yankees executive called Gehrig to schedule a private meeting with him in his Yankee Stadium office to discuss a baseball contract, eventually offering the prospect a spot in the organization. Gehrig signed a contract on April 30 and was at that moment and forevermore a New York Yankee.

Barrow's reason for signing Gehrig was based largely on his offensive potential. However, it went deeper than that: he was impressed with how Gehrig responded to his questions, believed he was sincere, appreciated his humility, and trusted his scout's evaluation of the Ivy Leaguer. "He was humble," former Yankee skipper Bill Virdon said, a quality often in short supply among ballplayers today.[1] That humility lasted throughout his career, no matter how well the slugger performed and how much in demand he eventually became.

By signing the young man to his first baseball contract, Barrow had instantly changed the fortunes of Gehrig and his parents, ensuring that Mom and Pop Gehrig would be able to live out their days with financial security and comfort. The player would never forget it. It also initiated a friendship with the Yankees executive that would continue until Gehrig's death, one he acknowledged in his "Luckiest Man" speech.

Gehrig's signing not only had immediate and long-term on-field implications to the Yankees; it also had an impact on the organization as it exists today and on Gehrig's retirement speech, in which he stated to the 62,000 Yankees faithful who were crowded into their home stadium that day, howling and cheering in support of their dying hero, that it was an honor to have known *"the builder of baseball's greatest empire, Ed Barrow."*

Figure 6.1. Ed Barrow, 1903.

Sixteen years later, Barrow would still be involved in Gehrig's service to the Yankees. Although Lou Gehrig Appreciation Day marked the unofficial end of Gehrig's career despite the fact that he hadn't played in a single game in two months but continued to wear a Yankees uniform and travel with the team, there was one thing left for Barrow to do in support of his slugger. He graciously retired Gehrig's uniform number, the first time any team had done that for any player in the history of major-league baseball. In addition to christening Gehrig as the first ballplayer to have his number retired, the action ensured that Gehrig, the first Yankee to wear the number four, would be the only player in the team's storied history to wear that numeral on his pinstripes.

While it started strong with Gehrig's signing, the Barrow-Gehrig relationship may have floundered briefly in 1932 as the Great Depression stretched its tentacles throughout the country and the bottom lines of teams began to suffer due to lagging attendance. With the organization's own attendance down a whopping 21 percent in 1932, the Yankees and Barrow asked Gehrig to accept a $2,000 pay cut by offering him $23,000 for the upcoming season despite the fact that he had hit an impressive forty-six home runs, knocked in 185 runners, and batted .341 in 1931. The low-key Gehrig didn't argue the matter—at that point he had too much respect for Barrow and the Yankees organization to let money come between them.

By 1938, with the Depression still lingering, things between the two had softened. After starring in *Rawhide*, Gehrig returned home with a large-caliber handgun he had purchased during his stay out west. While Gehrig had no known plans to use the weapon, he did apply for an obligatory gun permit in the state of New York. Of all the people he might have used as a reference, Gehrig chose Barrow, underscoring the faith he had in the Yankees chief executive. He could have asked his best friend, Bill Dickey; one of his father figures, Joe McCarthy or Jacob Ruppert; his own parents; or anyone else he considered a friend to vouch for his credibility, but he didn't. It was Barrow, the man who had effectively transformed his life fifteen years earlier, whom Gehrig trusted to provide an accurate appraisal of his gun worthiness.

Another pay cut was offered following the 1938 season, when Gehrig hit twenty-nine home runs, drove in 114 RBI, and hit .295 during what was clearly an off season for him. With barely a whimper from his star, who was far from satisfied with his own performance, Barrow sliced Gehrig's salary from $39,000 down to $36,000. Even with the nearly 10 percent salary decrease, the two men maintained a healthy and respectful relationship, each mindful of the impact the Depression was having on baseball fans as a whole and on everyone else around the country. Besides, Gehrig may have sensed that he deserved a cut in pay based upon his significant falloff in production from 1937 to 1938, even though he had a respectable season. Something seemed physically wrong with him; Gehrig knew it, and he took full responsibility for his statistical malaise by accepting the salary reduction without complaining. In the end, in some odd way, the salary drop may have reflected Barrow's affinity for Gehrig as both a person and a baseball player: the first baseman had expected an even heftier cut than the one his boss had proffered.

"He regarded Lou, in his own icy way, as an adopted son," the author Ray Robinson wrote of Barrow in his book *Iron Horse*.[2]

Through everything, the grueling streak of consecutive games played continued on, to Barrow's pleasure and apparent pride in the seemingly indestructible first baseman. There were even reports that sometime during the 1930s Barrow postponed a scheduled game due to anticipated rain at Yankee Stadium in order to give Gehrig an extra day of rest that would enable him to continue his streak with renewed fervor. On that day, as the entire team rested along with their star first baseman, blue skies shone above.

∽

Edward Grant Barrow entered a fast-changing post–Civil War world on May 10, 1868, in Springfield, Illinois, the eldest of four sons produced by John and Effie Barrow. He was born in a covered wagon during the Reconstruction period as his family traveled west to Nebraska in hopes of settling down on the Great Plains; they eventually backtracked and planted roots near Des Moines, Iowa, around 1874. Ten years later, at the tender age of sixteen, Barrow began working for a small community newspaper, managing a cadre of newsboys and rising through the organization to become head of the paper's modest circulation department. He enjoyed baseball immensely, however, and young Ed soon found himself playing on a local team as his time away from the newspaper permitted. He eventually suffered a serious arm injury while pitching during cool weather, and the boy was forced to seek other ways to express his interest in the game he loved. That didn't take long. In the 1890s Barrow began organizing and promoting his own ball clubs while working as a team manager, recruiting the newsboy and future Hall of Famer Fred Clarke for one of his clubs. As the owner of a team in Paterson, New Jersey, Barrow also signed future Hall of Famer Honus Wagner to a contract shortly before the turn of the century. Clarke and Wagner would be the first of numerous talented players whom Barrow would snag for his teams over the next half century. Easily among the most talented was Gehrig.

In time, Barrow was named to head the Atlantic League, and he soon bought a Canadian team in the Eastern League prior to the Detroit Tigers appointing him manager in 1903. Although he resigned less than two seasons into the job, Barrow continued to invest in minor-league organizations before being named to head the International League. Seven years later, in 1918, Barrow hit the jackpot and was signed to manage the respected Boston Red Sox, whose roster included a player whom Barrow would later come to know quite well: Babe Ruth. Barrow's Red Sox won the World Series in his first season with the club; however, after that things were all uphill in Beantown for the up-and-comer.

While he only remained with the Red Sox for three seasons, finishing first, sixth, and fifth between 1918 and 1920, Barrow's legacy is wrapped around a key decision he made during his final year with the team: he converted Boston pitching ace Ruth, a former twenty-four-game winner, into a slugging outfielder and one of the finest hitters ever to grace a batter's box. When the Yankees purchased Ruth from the financially struggling Red Sox in 1920, Barrow went along with him as the team's chief executive, eventually rising to become president of the organization when Ruppert died in 1939 just months before Gehrig's unanticipated exit from baseball; he remained with the Yankees in various capacities for twenty-six seasons. While Barrow was sowing his seeds of success early on with the Yankees, Ruth slugged fifty-four home runs in his first full season wearing pinstripes.

In all, Barrow managed five seasons in the big leagues—two with Detroit and three with Boston, finishing with a 310–320 record and a lackluster .492 winning percentage. Between 1896 and 1910 he also managed minor-league organizations in Wheeling, West Virginia; Paterson, New Jersey; Toronto and Montreal, Canada; and Indianapolis, Indiana. As 1920 came into view, his executive training period was effectively over.

It was in New York where Barrow experienced his greatest success as a baseball executive, due primarily to the elite skills of two of the greatest managers ever, Huggins and McCarthy, and the able hitting of three predominant sluggers: Ruth, Gehrig, and DiMaggio, all of whom he personally brought on board. With Huggins or McCarthy at the helm, there was little likelihood that Barrow or the Yankees would fail.

"Under Ed Barrow, one of the most complex and infinitely the most efficient baseball business firms ever operated was a one-man organization," wrote famed sportswriter Red Smith of the *New York Times*. "And its central office was under Ed's hat."[3]

With Barrow at the helm the Yankees won a total of fourteen pennants—eleven with Gehrig in the lineup at first base; those pennants translated to ten world championships. Since Barrow's retirement from the Yankees three-quarters of a century ago, the team has won a total of seventeen additional World Series titles.

In 1939, after doctors released information on Gehrig's faltering health to the Yankees, who in turn handed it over to the news media, Barrow did Gehrig a well-intentioned favor, although some might argue it deprived him of the right to know his true prognosis as an ALS sufferer. At some point it became apparent to those around him that the disease afflicting Gehrig might eventually claim his life. Eleanor knew the truth, as did a small circle of other people—including Barrow. However, Gehrig steadfastly maintained that he might one day recover from the disease that was sapping him of his coordination and strength and sending him spiraling downhill in an unmistakable fashion. In light of Gehrig's persistent hope, Barrow never divulged to him the true seriousness of his condition, even though it might have enabled him to live out his remaining years much differently.

Months later, when Lou Gehrig Appreciation Day came around, Barrow spared no expense in presenting a first-class sendoff for his big first baseman. He ordered that bunting be hung around the stadium in celebratory fashion and invited players from the world champion 1927 Yankees—Gehrig had been MVP that season—to attend the doubleheader, covering the travel costs for players who would arrive from outside New York City. Despite Barrow's hoopla, Gehrig anticipated the event with dread. As he stepped from the dugout prior to addressing the crowd, one man held his arm with both hands in a likely show of support: Barrow. His appearance on the field with Gehrig that day spoke volumes about his relationship with the first baseman—it was the first time that Barrow had publicly set foot on Yankee Stadium turf in nearly two decades.

At around Christmas that same year, Barrow announced that Gehrig's number had been retired. He didn't stop with that kindness, however. Barrow also announced that no player would ever again use Gehrig's locker, effectively retiring that as well. In one fell swoop it was made clear that Gehrig would remain, at least symbolically, a member of the Yankees family forever, if only by virtue of those two acts. "We always want Lou to feel he is still one of us and that he will always be welcome to use his locker whenever he wants to," said Barrow.[4]

As Gehrig's disease progressed and Eleanor struck up a correspondence with Dr. Paul O'Leary, who had served as an intermediary between the Mayo Clinic and other high-profile patients, Barrow graciously consented for O'Leary to contact the slugger's wife by sending his letters to Barrow's home address. Barrow in turn would quietly pass them along to Eleanor. It was doubtless an inconvenience for the increasingly responsible executive, who by then was president of the Yankees, to pass along the correspondence to Gehrig's wife, but he was happy to do it to circumvent the possibility of Gehrig intercepting the letters, which might shatter his hope for an eventual recovery. It was clear from O'Leary's letters that Gehrig's plight was a serious one, and Barrow performed an intended kindness by helping to shield him from the truth of his predicament in order to preserve his optimistic attitude and hope for recovery, misguided as that decision may have been. As his health worsened and Gehrig became more and more confined to his home, Barrow visited him often.

Toward the end, Gehrig and Barrow's friendship remained warm and strong. They dined together with their wives, frequently visited each other at home, and talked for extended periods, and Gehrig sought out Barrow for guidance regarding personal matters, dropping in to see him at Yankee Stadium or at his office on Forty-Second Street. Gehrig knew he could depend upon Barrow for anything at any time, and Barrow, considered one of the family by the slugger's parents, must have felt the same. They'd had their disagreements over contracts, but the strength of their friendship overcame that.

Throughout baseball history, many fine general managers have graced the front offices, although it's difficult to find many comparable to Barrow. In 2015, Society for American Baseball Research members Dan Levitt and Mark Armour compiled a list of their top twenty-five general managers of all time.[5] Heading the list is longtime Brooklyn Dodgers and St. Louis Cardinals executive Branch Rickey, a Hall of Famer. In a career that spanned several generations, Rickey's teams won eight pennants and four World Series titles, each of those championships with the Cardinals. He is also credited with developing baseball's farm system and, perhaps most important, signing Jackie Robinson to break baseball's color barrier.

Second on the list is Pat Gillick, who won three world championships—two with the Toronto Blue Jays and one with the Philadelphia Phillies.

In third place, behind Rickey and Gillick, is Barrow, with ten world championships to his credit, more than twice the number that Rickey won and three times that of Gillick. It's hard to argue that Barrow wasn't the greatest general manager ever and, as Gehrig expressed in his "Luckiest Man" speech, *"the builder of baseball's greatest empire."* It's an empire that continues to stand stronger than any other, and, in the minds of many, Barrow's role in its establishment elevates him near the top spot on anyone's list of all-time great general managers. Gehrig knew it, and he thanked him for that and for the important role he played in his life in his "Luckiest Man" speech.

CHAPTER 7

GRAND LITTLE FELLOW

> To have spent six years with such a grand little fellow as Miller Huggins?
>
> —Lou Gehrig, "Luckiest Man" speech

It's a paradox, Gehrig's enduring description of his one-time field manager, the bantam Miller Huggins, in his "Luckiest Man" speech: *grand* yet *little* was how Gehrig described the man, nicknamed Mighty Mite for his ferocious desire to win. Huggins *was* a little man, measuring a wee five-foot-six and weighing a chintzy 120 pounds. By comparison, Gehrig was a giant at an even six feet and a sturdy 200-plus pounds. To him, everyone probably looked puny. Not everyone seemed grand all the time, however.

Take Ruth, for instance, with whom Gehrig maintained a high-profile estrangement for several years until moments before he would mention Huggins's name in the same breath as Yankees brass Jacob Ruppert, his teammate Bill Dickey, and the manager Joe McCarthy during his famous speech on Lou Gehrig Appreciation Day. Not always grand, either, was Ray White, the young hurler who hit Gehrig in the head with a pitched ball during an exhibition game in 1934, knocking the slugger unconscious but not causing in any serious damage. In a comment that apparently stemmed from an earlier near miss thrown in his direction by the fellow Columbia University alum, Gehrig condemned White to Hades shortly before the potentially franchise-changing beaning. Those were harsh words coming from the mild-mannered Gehrig, who, it seemed, liked—or at least tolerated—nearly everyone.

66 | Bronx Epitaph

Then there was Huggins, Gehrig's manager since his rookie season of 1923, the Yankees' dedicated, no-nonsense field general beginning three years after Ruppert purchased the club in 1915 and the man who would introduce Gehrig to the Yankees players during the young man's first experience at the team batting cage. There were reasons for Huggins's staying power, which resulted in a twelve-year tenure with the ball club, six American League pennants, and three world championships.

Clearly, Gehrig was one of those reasons. In large part because of Gehrig, Huggins had a knack for winning ball games, although he did so less frequently during five seasons managing the Cardinals—1913–1917—than

Figure 7.1. Miller Huggins. Library of Congress, George Grantham Bain Collection.

he did for the Yankees. While with the Cards he finished in third place twice and sixth, seventh, and eighth place once each. By comparison, in a dozen seasons at the helm of the Yankees the manager finished first on six occasions, second twice, third twice, fourth once, and a distant seventh one time. Those first-place finishes were substantially due to Gehrig—and, of course, Ruth.

"He's the most patient manager I ever knew," Gehrig once proclaimed of Huggins, who taught him the ins and outs of baseball and never backed off from supporting him during those early learning years. "He stuck with me and encouraged me and helped me. He is the best teacher I ever had the privilege of being with."[1]

It was Huggins who took a chance and replaced journeyman first baseman Wally Pipp with Gehrig on Tuesday, June 2, 1925, after Gehrig had accumulated only thirty-eight at bats during his first two "seasons" in the major leagues. He went on to slug twenty home runs that year and eventually set a major-league record for consecutive games played, one that would stand for more than half a century. Pipp, conversely, was traded to Cincinnati that same year and disappeared from baseball just three years later after fifteen seasons in the major leagues—eleven of them with the Yankees, who so easily cast him aside. The Pipp footnote and tales that he benched himself in favor of Gehrig due to a headache irritate former Yankees pitcher Gil Patterson, longtime minor-league pitching coordinator for the Oakland A's. After injuring his throwing arm in 1977, his only season in the majors, Patterson found himself out of baseball even faster than Pipp. "Rather than retell the Wally Pipp story, why not just say Lou got an opportunity and he took advantage of it?" Patterson asked rhetorically, referring to the likely false headache narrative. "Maybe Wally helped Lou in ways that no one will ever know."[2]

In 1926 Huggins took considerable heat from a *New York Times* sportswriter who accused him of rolling the dice and relying on unproven youngsters such as Gehrig in an effort to win the World Series that year, calling the Yankees manager a "baseball Bolshevik" for "betting the roll on flaming youth."[3] That criticism was premature. Two years later, the Yankees won the World Series in four games behind Gehrig's four home runs and Ruth's three dingers along with an astronomical .625 combined batting average. That success, the team's second consecutive World Series sweep, resulted in cries to break up the team, something Huggins matter-of-factly dismissed. "It is our desire to have a pennant winner each year indefinitely," Huggins said, perhaps somewhat defiantly but in his usual mild manner. "New York fans want championship ball and the Yankees can be counted on to provide it. We are prepared to outbid other clubs for young players of quality." Period.[4]

That was all right by Gehrig, who once described Huggins as the finest friend that anyone might have. "He talked to him about his mother and father, about his financial problems, gave him sound advice and endless encouragement," wrote Frank Graham, a reporter who frequently traveled with the team and who wrote a 1942 biography of Gehrig. "He already was exerting a tremendous influence on him, and in later years Lou could look back and realize that here was a man who had helped tremendously to fashion his life. A man whom he not only respected, but for whom he had a great and abiding affection."[5]

Gehrig confirmed their closeness by praising Huggins in his "Luckiest Man" speech, even though his former manager had died a decade earlier in 1929. Despite Huggins's absence at Yankee Stadium that day, Gehrig still remembered to acknowledge with one simple notation how his manager had impacted his life during the six-plus years he had played under him, especially during his younger years: "*such a grand little fellow as Miller Huggins.*" Huggins's passing had clearly affected him, just as the seasons he had spent playing for Huggins had impacted the Yankees organization.

Their relationship effectively began with a simple kindness, or perhaps a courtesy, that Huggins showed him when Gehrig arrived at Yankee Stadium for the first time. It was 1923, and the then backup first baseman shyly trailed behind Huggins as the two walked across the grass leading from the dugout to home plate and approached the batting cage, where Ruth and other high-octane veterans stood around watching.

"Hey, Wally, let the kid hit a few, will ya?" Huggins hollered over to the Yankees' longtime first baseman Pipp, who sooner than later would be replaced by Gehrig at the Yankees' right corner.[6] As Pipp graciously stepped aside, the youthful Gehrig grabbed a bat with "Babe Ruth" emblazoned on the barrel and approached the plate to face a long-forgotten batting practice hurler. Within seconds Gehrig was drilling pitches over the Yankee Stadium wall, much like Ruth so frequently did using the same piece of lumber. Suddenly, in an instant, the Bambino probably realized that Huggins had just unveiled to everyone his newfound competition as the league's premier home-run hitter. It had to excite him, but it also had to send chills.

Not that everything was kindness and laughter where Huggins and Gehrig were concerned. There was also positive discipline designed to

Figure 7.2. Miller Huggins greets Washington Senators player-manager Clyde Milan prior to a 1922 game. Library of Congress, National Photo Company Collection.

boost Gehrig's capital as a player while ensuring he remained a mainstay in the lineup. Early in his career, while playing against the Ty Cobb–led Detroit Tigers, Gehrig missed a cutoff throw and allowed a runner to score while Cobb sprinted to collect an extra base, prompting Huggins to yell at Gehrig, "Whatsa matter with you, Lou? Can't you learn to make that cutoff play? After this, it'll cost you."[7] By rebuking him, Huggins showed his concern for the young man and his hope that the obvious error would not be repeated and Gehrig would become a much better grounded ballplayer. It wasn't, and he did.

By 1926, just three years after joining the Yankees, Gehrig had become a polished veteran, a player who had received votes for the league's Most Valuable Player Award in 1925 and who would soon enough win the award in his own right, the first of two. In Huggins's eyes, his first baseman had developed into a team player and a man committed to helping the Yankees win pennants. He acknowledged as much: "Lou has become an influence to the entire team," Huggins praised Gehrig. "You get a player with that kind of spirit and it spreads like a contagion to the other players. He has come much faster than I dared to expect."[8] Huggins, given that astounding validation of the young slugger, was clearly well pleased with his first baseman, who in 1926 would emerge as a powerful hitter on one of the best teams in baseball. The following season, he would set the tenor by hitting in the coveted cleanup spot on perhaps *the* greatest team ever: the 1927 Yankees.

"[Lou was] a friend [of Huggins] from the day the boy first walked, awestruck, into the Yankees' clubhouse," wrote Graham.[9] That became eminently clear after Huggins took ill while kneeling on the Yankees dugout steps during a game and had to visit the dressing room. The club physician, noting Huggins's temperature was on the rise, packed him into a cab and had him driven to a local hospital, where he died suddenly on September 25, 1929. His passing sent Gehrig into a funk that would continue until the last out of the 1929 season had been recorded. Graham wrote,

> The dwindling days of the [1929] season meant nothing to Lou. He didn't care whether he hit the ball or didn't, nor who won or lost a game. For the first time in his life there was no joy in going to the ball park each day, and the end of the season came as a relief. Now, at least, he would not have to see the battered roll-top desk where Hug had sat in the clubhouse nor miss his crouching figure on the dugout steps.[10]

Gehrig ended up with thirty-five home runs and 125 RBI but hit only .300 that season, his lowest batting average in three years.

As he would at the owner Ruppert's funeral years later, Gehrig served the memory of Huggins as a pallbearer along with Ruth. He accompanied

Huggins's body as it was transported back to the late manager's hometown Cincinnati, where it was buried in Woodlawn Cemetery.

∼

Miller James Huggins was born on March 27, 1878, in Cincinnati, Ohio, the son of a lifelong grocer and dedicated Methodist and the third of four offspring, including two brothers. His father, James, believed emphatically that children, especially his own, should behave properly, which might explain the serious demeanor his son demonstrated as an adult and particularly as a baseball manager. He probably inherited that seriousness from his father despite the influence of his mother, Sarah.

Growing up in southwest Ohio, the young Miller gravitated to baseball early on and by high school was captaining the Walnut Hills High School baseball team in Cincinnati; he also played on several local semiprofessional teams at about the same time, using the assumed last name "Proctor" in order to preserve his amateur status. In retrospect, the move—although a bit shifty—was one that proved propitious as Huggins moved along the baseball continuum, enabling him to play ball as an amateur in college.

Although the elder Huggins considered baseball somewhat frivolous, he didn't stop his son from participating in the sport. Eventually, father and son reached an early compromise by which Miller would play ball and study in relatively equal amounts. The deal paid solid financial dividends, as in 1899 the younger Huggins signed to play in the Interstate League with the Mansfield (Ohio) Haymakers. His playing name? Proctor.

From there, Huggins began to climb the baseball ladder, playing for the Fleischmann Mountain Tourists (New York) in 1900 while attending the University of Cincinnati Law School and playing on the college baseball team there. He then moved over to the St. Paul (Minnesota) Saints, where he hit .300 in both 1902 and 1903 and drew some interest from the hometown Cincinnati Reds, who eventually passed on him, allegedly because of his small, unimposing stature. While playing for the Saints he also managed the scorecard and food concessions as he pondered his next step within the baseball world, demonstrating that a baseball player could also succeed as an entrepreneur.

From St. Paul to the big leagues was just a short hop, and Huggins signed with the Reds the next year, in 1904. He immediately became the team's regular second baseman, playing in all but fourteen of the team's

154 games during his rookie season, collecting 129 hits, hitting two home runs, driving in thirty runners, and hitting a respectable .260. After one season in the major leagues Huggins had proved his skeptics—primarily the Reds—wrong: at five-foot-six, he really *could* make a go of things in the major leagues. Little did he know that would mean more than just hitting and throwing.

Never one to hit for power, Huggins put up numbers that were similar nearly each year after his rookie season and throughout his thirteen-year playing career. His high-water mark for home runs was two, which he accomplished twice (in 1904 and 1915), and he never drove in more than thirty-eight runners in a single season (1905). His lifetime batting average was only five points higher than his rookie mark of .265, and he hit a low of .214 in 1909.

After six seasons with Cincinnati, Huggins joined the Cardinals in 1910, where he once again performed solidly, if unspectacularly. He hit .304 during his third season in St. Louis, the best average of his career with the exception of his final season, when he was three for only nine at bats and hit .333. After the 1916 season, he hung up his spikes as a player in order to concentrate on managing.

From 1913 to 1916 Huggins wore two hats with the Cardinals, those of player and manager, finishing out of the money each season but honing his skills for what was to come later in New York. His best year managing in St. Louis was 1917, when the team went 82–70 and finished in third place. That was the only season Huggins managed the Cardinals as a nonplayer.

In 1918 Ruppert and the Yankees came calling on the recommendation of American League president Ban Johnson, and Huggins signed with the team against the wishes of Yankees co-owner Cap Huston, an adamant opponent of enlisting Mighty Mite and who instead wanted Wilbert Robinson of the Dodgers. Objecting, Ruppert bought out his partner, and Huggins was the man in whom the owner would place his faith as the Yankees began their quest for a first American League pennant.

Under Huggins, who replaced "Wild Bill" Donovan following a sixth-place finish in 1917, the Yankees finished in fourth place, three games under .500. While this was not a finish that Ruppert necessarily cheered, he nonetheless stood pat with the littlest general in his Yankees army. After third-place finishes in 1919 and 1920, Huggins won his first pennant for the Yankees in 1921 and followed that up with two more in succession and the organization's first world championship, in 1923—

Gehrig's first season in the majors. A dynasty had been born, although few knew it at the time.

After a two-year hiatus following the back-to-back-to-back pennants of 1921–23, Huggins brought home three more between 1926 and 1928 as well as two world championships. In his final year as manager of the Yankees, his final year of life, Huggins finished an incomplete season with an 82–61 record, and the Yankees ended up a respectable second in the American League. It wasn't the finish that Huggins would have wanted, but it was a successful season in which Ruth hit forty-six home runs and Gehrig thirty-five.

In the six seasons he played under Huggins, Gehrig seldom let him or the team down, never in a meaningful way. While he might miss a cutoff throw on occasion, or perhaps strike out with runners on base in a tight situation, or even get thrown out stealing with the ball game on the line, when it came to good, old-fashioned integrity, Gehrig had it in spades. Huggins knew that, as did Gehrig's teammates—even those who secretly begrudged him for his straight moral compass, something Huggins had to appreciate as Gehrig labored under the shadow of the happy-go-lucky Ruth. In Huggins's eyes, the two were like night and day.

"I guess I'll miss him more than anyone else," Gehrig said after Huggins's passing. "Next to my mother and father, he was the best friend a boy could have. When I first came up he told me I was the rawest, most awkward rookie he'd ever seen or come across in baseball. He taught me everything I know."[11] Put simply, Gehrig cherished the years he had spent with the "*grand little fellow*" Miller Huggins, as he fondly noted in his "Luckiest Man" speech.

CHAPTER 8

THE GREATEST MANAGER

> To have spent the next nine years with that master psychologist, the greatest manager in baseball today, Joe McCarthy?
>
> —Lou Gehrig, "Luckiest Man" speech

With a whisper in his ear and a pat on the back, Joe McCarthy coaxed his big first baseman toward a bevy of microphones situated on a swath of loose dirt near home plate at Yankee Stadium. Lou Gehrig wanted to resist his manager's inveiglement, a loving gesture perhaps aimed at securing the slugger's place in history. But who could forbear the legendary McCarthy's wishes?

It was July 4, 1939, and the mood on the playing field had been light that day, at least, somewhat light—as light as the darkness of a death sentence could allow. There was Gehrig, gifts sprinkled around home plate like Easter eggs, players and Yankees personnel mingling about, the crowd growing restless, microphones standing at attention.

For a while at least, things on the field were festive. A vigorous marching band trod the well-groomed infield in double time, playing the German song "Du, du liegst mir im Herzen" (translated loosely as "You are in my heart"). In fuzzy videos pocked with grain, Gehrig offers a relaxed smile and glances around the Yankee Stadium infield, cap in hand, clapping along with the crowd.

When Babe Ruth rose to address the uneasy throng—the two sluggers had been virtually estranged for half a decade until a hug that day melted the ice—things turned somber. The band played "I Love You Truly" as

Gehrig stared down, nervously pawing at the ground as the estrangement disappeared into dust. He and the Babe were at last copacetic, but what about everything else?

When the speeches were over, when Mayor La Guardia, Postmaster James Farley, Ruth, and McCarthy were finished paying their heartfelt respects to Gehrig, the journalist Sid Mercer thanked the crowd for coming out to the ballpark. Gehrig was off the hook, it seemed. Or was he?

As he turned to walk away, suddenly there was McCarthy, Gehrig's manager since 1931 and a father figure who had lost his own dad as a young child. It was McCarthy whom Gehrig had first contacted at the Book-Cadillac Hotel in Detroit (now the Westin Book Cadillac) on May 2, 1939, when, after 2,130 consecutive games played, he could no longer perform up to his own high standards of athleticism. At that moment, he knew it was time to quit—not only the streak but baseball itself. After nearly fourteen seasons without missing a game, Gehrig was suddenly and inexplicably through. "Joe, I'm out of the lineup," Gehrig had told McCarthy. "I'm just not doing the team any good."[1]

Two months later, on Gehrig's special day, his manager publicly and unequivocally repudiated the notion that Gehrig wasn't helping the team. Even a sick and slumping Gehrig was a significant benefit, if only to the team's morale, he implied. "Lou, what else can I say except that it was a sad day in the life of everybody who knew you when you came to my hotel room that day in Detroit and told me you were quitting as a ball player because you felt yourself a hindrance to the team," McCarthy told the slugger in front of 62,000 fans. "My God, man, you were never that."[2]

Then, as McCarthy coaxed his undisputed favorite player, it was Gehrig's turn. He seldom turned down anyone's request, and he certainly wouldn't start with McCarthy. Not on Lou Gehrig Appreciation Day, where McCarthy was so publicly appreciating him. With a heavy heart and fighting back tears, he strode toward home plate, delivering an unforgettable oration, one that would live forever.

"*Today I consider myself the luckiest man on the face of the earth*," he said, simply and eloquently. Thirteen prosaic words—magically delivered, wonderfully received, eternally preserved.

"That was a pretty profound statement," former Yankee catcher Rick Dempsey said of Gehrig's "luckiest man" declaration. "I don't think he could ever have said it any better. Gehrig had a total appreciation of baseball, the fans, New York, winning, playing every day—he was tough as nails. Then, looking death in the face and saying he was the luckiest

The Greatest Manager | 77

Figure 8.1. American League manager Joe McCarthy (*left*) shakes hands with National League manager Bill Terry before the 1937 All-Star Game in Washington, DC. Library of Congress, Harris & Ewing Collection.

man in the world, it's probably one reason why the New York Yankees are still the number one name in baseball."[3]

Next, in almost the same breath, Gehrig described McCarthy as a "*master psychologist, the greatest manager in baseball today.*" During McCarthy's twenty-four-year career managing three major-league teams, there were many notable accomplishments: he had won nine pennants for the Yankees and the Chicago Cubs. He had accumulated seven World Series titles, all of them with the Yankees—five with Gehrig embedded in the mix. More than 2,100 wins, an average of nearly ninety per season. A .615

lifetime winning percentage, first among top-tier managers. Membership in the coveted National Baseball Hall of Fame. Still, it was something McCarthy did on Lou Gehrig Appreciation Day that may have been his greatest accomplishment in a long career: standing near home plate alongside some of the greatest players to ever be assembled, including current and former teammates Bob Meusel, Tony Lazzeri, and Earle Combs, he convinced Gehrig to address the Yankee Stadium faithful—the *Lou Gehrig* faithful—and what Gehrig uttered were the most memorable words ever spoken on an athletic field. Those words also spawned a mystical thread that continues to wind through the organization today, noted ex-Yankee Dempsey. "Absolutely," he said of the historical connection, adding that as a member of the organization he perceived Gehrig's legacy thirty years after the player's death: "I felt the cry in the way they immortalized their players, and especially Gehrig."[4]

From the beginning, Gehrig's fondness for new manager McCarthy was evident, and he told his best friend as much in 1931: "You know, Bill," Gehrig told Dickey, "I like this McCarthy." It was mutual. "Lou had the same effect on [McCarthy] that he had on everyone he met, and McCarthy grew to look upon him as he might a son or a younger brother," wrote Gehrig biographer Frank Graham. "What a wonderful fellow that Gehrig was!" McCarthy once said. "Just went out every day and played his game and hit the ball."[5]

As the year progressed, it became clear that Gehrig's admiration was not misplaced; McCarthy had earned it. In turn, he respected Gehrig's solid work ethic and no-nonsense approach to the game and to life. He never pampered his players, and Gehrig appreciated that in a manager. The two had another bond: neither man had children. Perhaps that's why McCarthy favored Gehrig like a son. "McCarthy's supportiveness toward Lou . . . helped to bring Lou out of his shell," Ray Robinson wrote in his biography of Gehrig. "Praise from McCarthy for Lou was limitless."[6]

Graham agreed, writing that McCarthy had full confidence in Gehrig to always be in the lineup, to take good care of his body, and to represent the Yankees in a positive light at every opportunity. That was high praise from a man whom the players considered a strict disciplinarian, who used each athlete according to his ability and not based upon whether he liked him, who diligently worked his team into shape, and who managed every game—even exhibition games—to win. "Later, [their] relationship grew far beyond that of just a manager and a player," Graham wrote. "McCarthy was to become, as Huggins had been and Barrow continued to be, a man who had tremendous influence on Lou's life."[7]

~

Joseph Vincent McCarthy was born on April 21, 1887, in Philadelphia, Pennsylvania, the son of a building contractor. When the boy was only three his father died in a work-related cave-in, leaving the family impoverished and forcing young Joe to do what he could for himself and for his family: he shoveled dirt, carried ice, and did whatever was needed to help his mother.

One thing that wasn't impoverished was McCarthy's fondness for sports, specifically cricket and baseball, and he quickly developed a reputation in the cobblestone communities around Philadelphia as a capable ballplayer as early as grade school. Unfortunately for the budding star, he suffered a broken kneecap while playing ball as a boy, an injury that left the knee permanently damaged and likely kept him at a disadvantage later on as he struggled to make it to the big leagues. In the long run, it wouldn't matter. "It left me with a loose cartilage, which cut down on my speed," McCarthy said. "But I didn't do so good against a curved ball, either."[8]

In 1905 McCarthy enrolled at Niagara University on a baseball scholarship despite not having attended high school. He played two seasons of college ball, then left school in hopes of earning a living as a minor-league ballplayer. He broke in with the Wilmington Peaches in 1907 and later played for the Franklin Millionaires, the Toledo Mud Hens, the Indianapolis Indians, the Wilkes-Barre Barons (as player-manager), the Buffalo Bisons, and the Louisville Colonels (as player-manager and non-playing manager). In all, the well-traveled McCarthy played fifteen seasons in the minor leagues, the last seven with Louisville and the last eight at the double-A level. McCarthy finished his lengthy minor-league career with an inglorious thirty home runs—two per season—and a lifetime batting average of .261.

"In those early years in Louisville I became convinced that I never would set the woods on fire as a player," McCarthy once said. "My mind began to work along managerial lines. I studied the systems of successful managers of the period. My chance came midway through the 1919 season when Patsy Flaherty resigned."[9] McCarthy replaced Flaherty as manager of Louisville in midseason 1919.

While playing in Buffalo, New York, McCarthy, nicknamed "Marse Joe," had met an eligible bachelorette named Elizabeth "Babe" Lakeman, and the two were married in Louisville on February 14, 1921. Five years later, probably on the strength of his minor-league managerial successes in Wilkes-Barre and Louisville, the Chicago Cubs hired McCarthy as their new field boss, to lead a group of veterans that included future Hall of Famer Grover Cleveland Alexander. McCarthy promptly traded him away.

McCarthy spent five seasons with the Cubs, from 1926 to 1930, winning the National League pennant in 1929 but losing in the World Series to the Philadelphia Athletics despite achieving ninety-eight victories during the regular season. Largely because of the World Series loss, pressure mounted on McCarthy, and he resigned shortly before the 1930 season ended with the team in second place.

At about the same time, the sportswriter Joe Vila of the *New York Sun* called Yankees general manager Ed Barrow to recommend McCarthy for the managerial position that was open. Excited about the opportunity to join the Bronx Bombers, McCarthy threw his hat in the ring and was hired by Jacob Ruppert.

"I have no illusions about the task ahead of me with the Yankees," McCarthy wrote at the time[10]—not that illusions would have prevented him from winning, as McCarthy went on to become one of the most successful managers in the history of the game. After fifteen seasons with the Yankees, McCarthy finished out his managerial career guiding the Boston Red Sox for three seasons before retiring from the game in 1950.

After half a century, McCarthy was gone from the game he loved but was certainly not forgotten. In 1957, just seven years after he retired from baseball, the National Baseball Hall of Fame's Veterans Committee voted McCarthy into that select fraternity of players and managers. After that, he lived quietly on a farm he owned for the next twenty-one years until his death from pneumonia in Buffalo on January 13, 1978. McCarthy, who was ninety when he died, was interred at Mount Olivet Cemetery in Tonawanda, New York. He is buried next to his wife, Babe—the most important Babe in his life.

Robinson notes McCarthy's affinity for Gehrig in his book *Iron Horse* as he describes an incident that occurred during the 1933 season. After Washington Senators second baseman Buddy Myer landed spikes down on Gehrig's heel in a play at second base, tempers flared. A fight ensued several days later after Yankee Ben Chapman, in apparent retaliation, slid spikes-up into Myer at second base. "It was Buddy who had committed the most unpardonable deed a man could perpetuate on a ball field: he had tried to inflict injury on McCarthy's favorite Yankee," wrote Robinson.[11]

By the following season, Ruth and Gehrig were barely speaking. There were several reasons for the duo's deteriorating relationship, but one of them involved McCarthy and his close relationship with Gehrig: Ruth apparently begrudged his teammate's adulation of the Yankees manager, which he didn't share. While Gehrig was on excellent terms with McCarthy both personally and professionally, Ruth, his skills by then slipping, was not. The result was increasing resentment that carried through to Lou Gehrig Appreciation Day.

On July 14, 1934, it was McCarthy who graciously saved Gehrig's consecutive games streak on at least this one occasion. Suffering from lumbago (or perhaps the onset of ALS) and a bad cold, Gehrig notified his manager that he'd not be able to play that day. Enjoying his first baseman's streak almost as much as Gehrig was, McCarthy wouldn't hear of it. He helped dress his star, hauled him over to a waiting cab, and carried him from the taxi to the stadium, where players helped their teammate into his uniform. McCarthy then penciled Gehrig into the leadoff position, where he batted once before leaving the game. The streak was intact.

Perhaps most poignant was his appearance alongside Gehrig prior to the "Luckiest Man" speech, where McCarthy described his friend as "the finest example of ball player, sportsman, and citizen that baseball has ever known."[12] Then, in an unabashed expression of his love and admiration for Gehrig, McCarthy broke down and openly sobbed, embracing his ailing star.

Mike Buddie, who pitched for the Yankees from 1998 to 1999, experienced firsthand the inspiration wrought by Gehrig. Said Buddie, "As a relief pitcher, anytime I walked to the bullpen or retrieved a ball hit over the fence I passed through Monument Park," an open-air museum in Yankee Stadium where plaques, retired numbers, and monuments memorializing and honoring distinguished Yankees, many of them deceased, are displayed. "When you see Lou Gehrig and Babe Ruth and Mickey Mantle [represented], it resonates."[13]

Over the eight years the two were together as player and manager, Gehrig and McCarthy developed a strong bond. When Gehrig died, McCarthy was notified as he exited a cab near the Yankees' hotel. He was stunned. Days later at Gehrig's funeral, it wasn't enough for the veteran manager to simply walk past his coffin, smile affectionately, and nod his approval. Instead, he reached over into the casket and shook Gehrig's lifeless hand as a farewell gesture to his friend and an acknowledgement of a job well done and a life well lived. Gehrig was gone, and McCarthy's life as well as the Yankees organization had suddenly changed forever.

Of the fourteen full seasons that Gehrig played in the major leagues, all of them with the Yankees, just over half occurred under McCarthy's watchful and almost parental eye. If statistics are any indicator, Gehrig displayed the full measure of his ability under the man who considered him a son. From 1925 through 1930, Gehrig hit 243 doubles, compared with 286 under McCarthy, and 186 home runs, compared with 306 with McCarthy as manager. Without a doubt, McCarthy brought out the best in his famous slugger, and Gehrig wouldn't have had it any other way. His acknowledgment of McCarthy in his famous speech was a lasting tribute to a great friend, dedicated father figure, Hall of Fame manager, and "*master psychologist, the greatest manager in baseball today.*"

"They were seemingly made for each other," Jonathan Eig wrote in his Gehrig biography, adding, "Gehrig loved rules. When his manager or his mother didn't provide them, he constructed and enforced his own. He played each game as if it were the most important of his life . . . He sulked when he lost, brooded when he slumped, and turned a cold shoulder to teammates who didn't play as hard as he thought they could. He quickly became his manager's favorite player."[14] That feeling, it appeared, was mutual, and Gehrig had no hesitation about letting his fans and the world know it as he exited baseball forever.

CHAPTER 9

MY ROOMMATE

> And when you have the privilege of rooming, eating, playing cards, and knowing one of the greatest fellows that ever lived, my roommate, Bill Dickey.
>
> —Lou Gehrig, "Luckiest Man" speech

They were, it seems, two peas in a pod—Lou Gehrig and his pal Bill Dickey. For starters, Gehrig played sixteen seasons in the major leagues, all of them with the New York Yankees, compared with Dickey's seventeen years wearing Yankees pinstripes. Dickey was an All-Star eleven times, while Gehrig made the squad seven times, although the All-Star Game wasn't introduced until a decade after his career began. Gehrig cracked the top ten in balloting for the American League's Most Valuable Player Award a remarkable nine times to Dickey's five; Gehrig won that exclusive honor twice, and Dickey finished in second place once. Both recorded lifetime batting averages well over .300: Gehrig hit .340 over his long career, and Dickey batted .313. Both were voted into the National Baseball Hall of Fame during their lifetimes—Gehrig in 1939, and Dickey in 1954.

For many years, Gehrig and Dickey were the best of friends, fraternally involved in each other's lives. How close were they?

The two probably met sometime in 1928 when Dickey was called up to the Yankees during Gehrig's sixth season with the ball club. Within five years Gehrig and Dickey had clearly become close, which was underscored when Gehrig and his wife were married in New York City during the early years of the Great Depression. The couple had originally planned to marry on September 30, 1933; however, out of frustration and perhaps on a whim, they moved the ceremony up a day due to family squabbles involving Gehrig's sometimes-meddlesome mother, whose officiousness had apparently cost her son other relationships with women. When the two did marry at their New Rochelle apartment on September 29, the modest ceremony was officiated by the mayor of New Rochelle, Walter C. G. Otto, who afterward led a motorcade to Yankee Stadium so that Gehrig could play in the final game of the regular season. Gehrig's mother was causing problems, Eleanor wrote years later: "[Lou] picked up the phone, called the mayor of New Rochelle and told him to bring the marriage license and make it fast. A little while later the mayor did exactly that, to the accompaniment of a covey of motorcycle cops escorting him."[1] A small reception was held the following afternoon, and Dickey was the only Yankee in attendance.

That same year, the Yankees released Gehrig's road roommate, Joe Sewell, at the end of the season. Sewell, a thirteen-year veteran who had joined the Yankees in 1931 after spending eleven years with the Cleveland Indians, would retire just one season after playing well enough to receive a few nods for the American League MVP Award in 1932. Sewell was quickly replaced as Gehrig's bunkmate by the Southerner Dickey, and the two roomed together for seven years. The catcher said later that the match was a good one as he and Gehrig shared many interests and got along quite well. "I was a close friend of Gehrig's long before I succeeded Joe Sewell as his roommate," Dickey said of the switch. "Lou and I liked to do the same things. We liked movies, same foods, same hours. We liked to talk baseball, we had similar ideas, we looked at life much in similar ways."[2]

The following season, in June 1934, Ray White's pitched ball struck Gehrig in the head, flattening him. As Gehrig lay sprawled on the dirt, Dickey raced out to assist his fallen teammate, helped him get oriented, and walked his friend back to the welcoming confines of the Yankees dugout, from where he'd be transported to a local hospital for examination and treatment.

On August 1, 1937, when Gehrig hit for the cycle for the second time in his illustrious career, there was cause for celebration by the Yankee first baseman. His performance against the St. Louis Browns was a rare one that most players only dream about achieving. Gehrig and Dickey celebrated the following day by going deep-sea fishing on the Maryland coast. Gehrig's best catch of the day, a marlin weighing in at nearly ninety pounds, was slightly smaller than the one Dickey caught—one of

Figure 9.1. Bill Dickey (*far right*) poses with Hall of Famer Joe Cronin (*center*) and Lou Gehrig in 1937. Library of Congress, Harris & Ewing Collection.

the few times that Dickey bested his best friend. (Another time was in 1936 when Dickey hit .362 compared with Gehrig's .354. Usually, it was Gehrig coming out on top.)

Two years later, in 1939, when Gehrig was notified by the Mayo Clinic that he was suffering from the disease that would eventually claim his life, Dickey was the first non-family member he told about his misfortune. His friend shed tears over the news.

Not that Dickey wasn't already suspicious that something was not quite right with Gehrig's health. After all, the two were roommates and nearly as close as spouses. As such, Dickey had seen Gehrig stumble for no apparent reason in recent weeks. He felt certain that something was seriously wrong.

"Dickey and Gehrig were close friends, and Dickey was the first teammate to know that Gehrig was ill," Thomas Rogers wrote for the *New York Times* in reporting Dickey's death in 1993. Rogers added, "Later, Dickey was the only active player to play himself in *Pride of the Yankees*, a movie about Gehrig."[3] Dickey was so close to Gehrig that he initially turned down the movie role, saying it would be too difficult for him to address Gary Cooper, who starred as Gehrig in the movie, as "Lou."

Not long after he contracted ALS, Gehrig's walking started to become unstable, and doctors suggested that in order to preserve his strength and overall health he curtail some of his regular activities, such as his work for the New York City Board of Parole. Dickey knew that his once-strapping friend was discouraged by the suggestion that he adopt a more leisurely lifestyle, and he was one of the faithful who frequently stopped by the Gehrig residence just outside the city to comfort and encourage the couple as they struggled to come to grips with Lou's ALS.

Lou and Eleanor eventually did come to grips with his disease, as much as that was possible. However, after Ed Barrow, the Yankees general manager, released to the news media the Mayo Clinic's report confirming that Gehrig had been diagnosed with ALS, the big first baseman sat beside his good friend in the team dugout prior to that day's ball game, probably for the comfort that he knew Dickey would provide during a difficult time. Dickey didn't let him down.

Then, when word came that Gehrig had died, Dickey, once again distraught, reportedly wept again. The two, who were seemingly inseparable in life, were at last separated by Gehrig's death.

"Lou was a gentleman, he was fun to be around," Dickey said many years later. "He was hard to get to know, but I've never seen a fella who loved baseball and loved to talk about it like Gehrig did."[4]

Just as Gehrig had been an honorary pallbearer at the late Yankees owner Ruppert's funeral two years earlier, so Gehrig was represented by honorary pallbearers at his own service, held at Christ Episcopal Church in the Bronx. It's not known whether Gehrig or his wife chose the honorees, but if Eleanor did, she would have known whom Gehrig preferred to stand for him. Those so named included Dickey—who had eaten breakfast with Gehrig the morning he asked McCarthy to pull him out of the lineup, something the two presumably discussed over eggs and flapjacks—as well as his manager Joe McCarthy and friend and motion-picture dancer Bill "Bojangles" Robinson.

A month after Gehrig's death, some 62,000 fans again congregated at Yankee Stadium, just as they had two years earlier on Lou Gehrig Appreciation Day, to memorialize their fallen slugger. Among those addressing the crowd on that day was a somber Dickey, humbled to eulogize his fallen friend. "This memorial to Lou Gehrig is a tribute of the Yankees to the greatest first baseman and pal in the history of the game," he said in an emotional delivery.[5]

Following Gehrig's untimely death and the country's entry into World War II just five months later with the attack on Pearl Harbor, Dickey purchased war bonds worth eight thousand dollars in remembrance of his friend, who, as a man of German lineage, had feared war ever since Adolph Hitler's ascendancy to power during the 1930s.

∽

Nicknamed "The Man Nobody Knows" due to his even temper and seeming aloofness, William Malcolm Dickey was born in Bastrop, Louisiana, situated 220 miles from New Orleans, on June 6, 1907, the son of a train conductor with the Missouri Pacific Railroad who was a fair semiprofessional baseball player. He was reared with his two sisters and two brothers, one of whom would also play major-league baseball, in the onetime railroad town of Kensett, Arkansas, and as a grade schooler Bill began palling around with future congressman Wilbur Mills, who remained a lifelong friend until their deaths a year apart. Dickey relocated with his family to Little Rock when he was sixteen years old, attending Searcy High School, and the capital city remained home to him for the rest of his life.

Thanks in part to his father's tutelage and encouragement, the quiet, slow-talking, well-designed young man played on the college football and baseball teams as a high school student attending Little Rock College, and he eventually began playing semipro baseball for a team based in Hot Springs, Arkansas, earning ten dollars per Sunday game. It wasn't long before major-league clubs began showing interest in the six-foot-one, 185-pound catcher. After signing with the Chicago White Sox at the age of only seventeen and playing three games for the team's Arkansas Travelers, Dickey was farmed out to Muskogee, Oklahoma, then returned to the Travelers, then was sent on to Jackson, Mississippi, where in 1927 the Yankees eventually purchased his contract for what was then a respectable twelve thousand dollars upon the recommendation of the scout Johnny Nee, who thought so highly of Dickey that he put his job on the line in a tongue-in-cheek fashion. "I will quit scouting if this boy does not make good," said Nee.[6] Fortunately for the Yankees and for Nee, the scout didn't have to. Instead, the team sent Dickey briefly to the minor leagues before he joined the big club in 1928, hitting .200 with a modest fifteen at bats and knocking in two RBI with a double and a triple during what for him was a short season. The next season was another story, as Dickey became a Yankee for keeps when he batted .346 with ten home runs.

Officially a rookie in his first full season and the team's regular catcher, the twenty-one-year-old Dickey suddenly found himself playing alongside the likes of Ruth, Gehrig, Meusel, and Lazzeri, stars he had only read about in newspapers and magazines and never dreamed he would someday meet. "Babe Ruth and Lou Gehrig were both my idols," Dickey said in a 1987 oral history interview for the National Baseball Hall of Fame. "I never saw two guys who could hit the ball out of the park in any direction like *they* could."[7]

After Dickey's call-up, Miller Huggins, who was then the manager, made it clear from the outset what his role would *not* be: "We pay one player here for hitting home runs and that's Babe Ruth," Huggins said, stating in certain terms that Dickey was not hired to hit for power. "So, choke up and drill the ball. That way you'll be around here longer."[8]

Choke up and drill he did, and in 1929, his first full season with the club, Dickey batted a reassuring .324 with ten home runs and sixty-five RBI. Needless to say, Yankee Stadium would be his residence for years to come.

During the seasons that followed, Dickey, as Huggins had suggested, hit more for average than for sock, batting .339, .327, .310, .318, and .322 between 1930 and 1934 before slumping briefly to .279 and then jumping back up to .362 in 1936, .332 in 1937, .313 in 1938, and .302 in 1939. During 1943, his final full season in the major leagues, Dickey hit an impressive .351 on the strength of 242 at bats, then entered military service. Unbeknownst to him, his days as a regular catcher were almost over.

Dickey spent two years out of baseball during World War II, then attempted to return as a player; however, his tenure was brief. McCarthy's resignation on May 24, 1946, cut that effort short partway through the season, and instead of returning to the team as a player, Dickey was named to replace his beloved manager, an assignment that would last only one season. When the Red Sox clinched the American League pennant several weeks before the season ended, Dickey resigned almost immediately. Although the Yankees finished in third place with a 57–48 record, his days of playing and managing in the major leagues were effectively over.

Interestingly, during the latter third of his career, Dickey's brother, George "Skeeter" Dickey, had a six-season major-league run with the Red Sox and the White Sox after first signing with the Yankees, batting .204 with four home runs and fifty-four RBI in eighty-three games. He retired in 1947, the year after his brother checked out of baseball with 202 home runs (despite choking up!), 1,209 RBI, and a lifetime batting average of .313, ranking him in the top one hundred of all time.

Bill Dickey may have retired from the major leagues as a player and manager, but he certainly was not out of baseball altogether. After managing for a year in Little Rock, he happily returned to the Yankees as first-base coach under the crusty, likable Casey Stengel, and he is credited with indoctrinating future Hall of Fame catcher Yogi Berra in the intricacies of catching.

When Dickey himself was inducted into the National Baseball Hall of Fame in 1954, he addressed the crowd in typical understated fashion. He called his induction "the nicest thing ever to happen to me."[9]

"He was a great catcher, great hitter, and a great man to have on the ball club," McCarthy once said of the personable, calm, and collected Dickey. "The records prove Dickey was the greatest catcher of all time."[10]

After Dickey left baseball, his brother, George, hired him to sell securities for a prominent investment banking firm in Little Rock; he held the position until 1977. On November 12, 1993, Dickey died at a Little Rock nursing home at the age of eighty-six. Six years later, the *Sporting News* named him the fifty-seventh greatest baseball player of all time. He failed to make the all-century team, nosed out by—who else?—Berra, the man whom Dickey had mentored.

"Bill Dickey is the best [catcher] I ever saw," said Hall of Fame pitcher Bob Feller. "He was as good as anyone behind the plate and better with the bat. There are others I'd include right behind Dickey, but he was the best all-around catcher of them all. I believe I could have won thirty-five games [during a season] if Bill Dickey was my catcher."[11]

Perhaps more important than Dickey's relationship to baseball was Gehrig's relationship to his friend, whom he described as "*one of the greatest fellows that ever lived.*" Seemingly all the major events in Gehrig's life after the two first met involved Dickey in some manner: Gehrig's marriage, his beaning, his fatal illness, his "Luckiest Man" speech, his death, and the eulogy at Yankee Stadium. While Gehrig and Dickey's teammates likely knew the depth of their friendship, Yankees fans probably did not, simply because the sportswriters who covered the team had little reason to discuss it in print and the media exposure that ballplayers received back then was not as intrusive as it is today.

Decades after Gehrig's death, Dickey recounted a second episode of signing autographs after disembarking from a train with his friend. As he and Gehrig took a cab to their hotel, Gehrig looked at him and said, "Look at all those kids having all that fun and here I am dying."[12]

Even more emotional for Dickey was Lou Gehrig Appreciation Day in 1939, which brought him to tears. "I believe that was the most emotional day that I've had in my life," he said.[13]

That emotion was fanned by Dickey himself. It was he who asked the writer John Kieran to pen the poem about Gehrig that was inscribed on the trophy presented to the Iron Horse at home plate that day. Gehrig treasured that poem, which echoed Dickey's personal sentiments about his ailing friend, more than any other gift he received on that trying day. Dickey's influence on the gift may have been why.

Several years before his death, Dickey, looking back nearly half a century, reflected on his former partner in baseball and other crimes: "What a guy and what a ballplayer," Dickey said, the years melting away.[14] By gratefully mentioning the Yankee catcher in his "Luckiest Man" speech, Gehrig expressed in no uncertain terms that he felt exactly the same way.

CHAPTER 10

ACROSS THE RIVER

> When the fellows from across the river, the New York Giants, a team you would give your right arm to beat, and vice versa, sends a gift, that's something. It's something to be remembered by a rival organization.
>
> —Lou Gehrig

There they were, propped at his feet near home plate in Yankee Stadium: a handful of trophies, gifts, and other remembrances symbolically glowing above the dust and intended to make Gehrig's transition from New York Yankee to terminally ill patient a little easier.

Not that he'd need most of those items in light of the significant health challenge that lay in front of him, except the trophy engraved with the names of his teammates, which he treasured until his death less than two years later and which probably inspired him, at least at some level, as he fought a losing battle with the crippling disease known as ALS. The trophy carried the poem penned by John Kieran, and it made Gehrig feel as though the previous seventeen seasons meant more to his teammates and the news media than simply 493 home runs, which had helped the team win seven World Series titles—including three over the rival Giants.

The other gifts, however, were less than practical, at least in the context of Gehrig's burgeoning life-and-death struggle, but reflected the affections of the Yankees, their staff, their concessionaires, and others. These included the loving cup and fishing pole paid for by his teammates, the tobacco stand, the scrolls, and the jewelry from the same company that made Gehrig's World Series bands.

Going forward, it was less than likely that the Gehrigs would be doing much, if any, formal entertaining, making the silver service set, the platters, and the pitcher he received somewhat impractical for occasional use, perhaps even obsolete. Nor would he do much high-energy deep-sea fishing, a hobby he shared with teammate and friend Bill Dickey, as his strength was diminishing. He did smoke, so the tobacco stand could occasionally prove useful; however, Gehrig's doctors may have recommended he not partake in tobacco in order to conserve his already-diminishing health for as long as possible. The scrolls and ring were thoughtful and kind and nice, but they probably received scant attention from Gehrig and his wife after they brought them back to their home along with everything else the slugger had received that day.

One set of gifts, however, appeared to mean something to Gehrig, or perhaps it was the giver that was important. Nowadays, a retirement such as his would have elicited gifts from nearly every team in both leagues as well as from the baseball commissioner, the presidents of the American and National leagues, and scores of other people, organizations, and peripheral entities. Not so during that era, or at least during the austere years of the Great Depression. However, two gifts, although modest in certain respects, apparently stood out in Gehrig's mind. The crosstown Giants, "*the fellows from across the river*" who had battled the Yankees for decades, swapping pennants and World Series titles, sent over a pair of candlesticks and a fruit bowl. Nothing special from a cost standpoint, but no other team is known to have contributed a gift on Gehrig's special day. The club's thoughtfulness was certainly important to the ailing ballplayer as he bid adieu to the lifestyle that had been so important to him and prepared for a new season of life.

Gehrig probably knew whom each gift was presented by prior to the ceremony. He was aware the Giants had contributed, and in the emotion of that moment, speaking from his broken heart rather than the written notes he had compiled the night before but in the end appeared not to follow, he still remembered to acknowledge the Giants in his speech. Only one team was mentioned that day, and, if nothing else, the Giants—who nineteen years later would move away from New York and across the country to San Francisco, driving a stake through the heart of their longtime rivalry with the Yankees—would live on in history for that one special kindness offered to a seriously ill man who desperately needed kindnesses at that particular moment.

"*When the fellows from across the river, the New York Giants, a team you would give your right arm to beat, and vice versa, sends you a gift, that's something,*" Gehrig told the crowd. "*It's something to be remembered by a rival organization.*"

Why did the rival Giants, and only the Giants, provide gifts for Gehrig, though modest ones?

First and foremost, Gehrig was a native of New York, home to both teams, and although the slugger was a longtime nemesis whose Yankees had beaten the Giants and their managers John McGraw (1923) and Bill Terry (1936 and 1937) in three World Series over a fourteen-year period, he *was* a member of the New York fraternity of major-league baseball players, which at that time was second to few other, if any, societies of athletes in the entire world. As such, he was, in a way, one of *them*. Terry, who would go to any reasonable length to beat the dreaded Yankees, especially during the World Series, realized that about Gehrig—the two were considered rivals and among the best first basemen around—and he appreciated the man for what he had accomplished in the name of New York baseball. A surprise gift—candlesticks and a fruit bowl—was the least the Giants could do to acknowledge Gehrig's many contributions to a sport that every player on the Giants team loved and reaped financial rewards from, including the great Terry himself. The gift may also have been Terry's way of thanking Gehrig for spurring him on to his own greatness as a first baseman during his Hall of Fame career.

Perhaps it went deeper than that, however, way back to the summer of 1921 following Gehrig's graduation from high school. His performance during the inter-city high school baseball championship had elevated the young man's stature beyond New York City, and prior to Gehrig's enrollment at Columbia a Giants scout named Arthur Irwin had approached Gehrig and suggested he try out for the team.

Irwin informed Gehrig that McGraw, who had managed the club since the year before Gehrig was born and was then in his twenty-second season at the helm, had watched him play and had interest in signing the young man to a baseball contract. Whether that was true and McGraw simply had second thoughts later on is lost to the ages. What *is* known is that things didn't work out as Gehrig had hoped, and the contract never materialized. He left the Polo Grounds deeply disappointed.

Figure 10.1. Longtime New York Giants manager John McGraw (*right*) poses with Babe Ruth, 1923. Library of Congress, George Grantham Bain Collection.

"I have often thought [that] because of later developments, if he had given me a real opportunity to make good and taken pains with me, the baseball situation in New York perhaps would have been a lot different in the years that were to come," Gehrig once said.[1]

Might the culture of excellence that persists today, "the baseball situation in New York," as Gehrig put it, have begun with him, Babe Ruth, and some of the other early Yankees stars? "It very well could have," said former Yankee Andy McGaffigan.[2]

Gehrig was certainly encouraged by Irwin's interest, and, buoyed by his family's need for additional income as they struggled to make ends meet, he tried out for the team at the Yankees' former ballpark and the Giants' then home field, the Polo Grounds, after the final game of the 1921 season. Unbeknownst to Gehrig, McGraw had apparently *not* previously watched Gehrig play and *not* promised Irwin he might sign the youth to a contract as the scout had indicated. That might have changed when Gehrig belted seven home runs that day, attracting the interest of all those who were watching, including the manager. However, McGraw's interest apparently dissipated when Gehrig allowed a ground ball to trickle between his legs.

"Get this fellow out of here!" McGraw demanded of no one in particular. "I've got enough lousy players without another one showing up."[3]

Gehrig left the ballpark understandably disillusioned by McGraw's exhortation; however, the Giants scout Irwin was not one to give up easily—not where a potential can't-miss signee was concerned. He enthusiastically offered Gehrig a contract with the team's Class A Hartford Senators in the Eastern League for the remainder of the 1921 season, a contract that Gehrig happily accepted. He played twelve games for the Senators using two poorly concocted aliases: Lou Lewis and Lefty Gehrig. He hit a respectable .261.

Although Gehrig claimed he was told that playing for Hartford wouldn't cause problems with his college eligibility, the venture was clearly a ruse on someone's part since false names were used. The ruse was eventually discovered, forcing Gehrig's coach to contact each of Columbia's rival schools and any possible future rivals to request that their teams and their coaches forgive Gehrig for what appeared to some an innocent indiscretion. While fortunately not expelled, Gehrig was forced to sit out his entire freshman season, postponing his eligibility until the fall of 1922. In doing so, the halfback-lineman-punter on the football team and pitcher-first baseman-outfielder on the baseball team learned a valuable lesson, as McGraw had for not signing Gehrig to a Giants contract in the first place. Years later, after Gehrig became successful with the Yankees, McGraw undoubtedly recalled the incidents—including the slugger's tryout and his later suspension at Columbia, not to mention Gehrig himself—with an element of regret, and he eventually called Gehrig the greatest first baseman ever. As successor to McGraw beginning in 1932, Terry was likely aware of the legendary manager and Gehrig's early history together, and it may have amused him. It also may have led to the Giants offering the gift as a final gesture of goodwill.

Figure 10.2. Members of the New York Giants, a frequent nemesis of the Yankees during the 1920s and 1930s, mill around a batting cage, 1923. Library of Congress, George Grantham Bain Collection.

When the 1923 World Series rolled around, McGraw may have had some misgivings about not having offered Gehrig a contract in 1921. Hoping to play for the Yankees during the series was none other than Gehrig, the man described by McGraw as "lousy" just two years earlier. Gehrig wouldn't play due to a slight by McGraw. Was it sour grapes on the part of the Giants manager? Or was it simply the man's competitive spirit? It was probably a little bit of both.

During 1923, the rookie Gehrig had played in only thirteen games, all of them late in the season. In order to be eligible for World Series play, any player who was called up late needed approval from the commissioner—in this case, Kenesaw Mountain Landis. Landis had granted his approval to Gehrig, but he told the Yankees they also needed approval from the opposing manager, McGraw. McGraw's Giants had beaten the Yankees in both the 1921 and 1922 World Series, and the manager, nicknamed Little Napoleon for good reason, wasn't about to have the streak end on the heroics of a young player whom he'd let slip through his fingers two years earlier. In a second snub, he declined to allow Gehrig to play—giving the Yankees good reason to dislike the Giants manager.

Perhaps it was fitting, but without Gehrig in the Yankees lineup or available to play coming off the bench, the team, under the guidance of Miller Huggins, still beat the Giants in the 1923 World Series, 4–2. What an uplifting way to christen Yankee Stadium just six months after it opened.

The teams would not meet again in the World Series until 1936, and that time Gehrig would certainly play. He would blast two home runs, slug a double, punch five singles, and bat an acceptable .292 for the series, which the Yankees again won by a 4–2 margin.

The following season, 1937, marked the final time the Yankees and Giants would meet in the postseason classic with Gehrig in the mix. Although aging and perhaps even showing slight signs of the ALS that would force his retirement just two years down the road and ultimately take his life, he hit .284 with one home run, a triple, a double, and two singles. He also drove in three runs.

The point had been made. The man whom McGraw had allowed to escape the Giants' net had come back to bite the team for a second World Series. And although McGraw had been replaced as manager by future Hall of Famer Terry, himself a lifelong Giant, one thing was clear: the man whose inaction had allowed Gehrig to sign with the Yankees had significantly enhanced the Yankees' fortunes, and Terry had to respect that. Perhaps that's why the Giants sent a gift to him on Lou Gehrig Appreciation Day—it may have been the team's way of apologizing.

One irony: On June 3, 1932, McGraw announced his retirement from baseball after thirty seasons playing for and managing the Giants. That same day, Gehrig achieved one of the rarest of all offensive feats in baseball when he hit four home runs in a 20–13 victory over the Philadelphia Athletics; he became the first player in the modern era ever to hit four home runs in a single game. The McGraw announcement captured headlines in newspapers around the country, while Gehrig's rousing performance was relegated to smaller articles in the same publications. Even in retirement McGraw had one-upped Gehrig.

Although McGraw had slighted Gehrig on at least two occasions, when all was said and done, he, Gehrig, and Terry had much in common. Gehrig and McGraw both played seventeen seasons in the major leagues, while Terry played fourteen. Gehrig and Terry each played with only one team throughout their careers, while McGraw played with four. The lifetime batting averages of all three were comparable: Terry hit .341 compared with Gehrig's .340 and McGraw's .334. If there's camaraderie in achieving like statistics, and if camaraderie creates goodwill, then perhaps the hitting successes of McGraw and Terry played a minor role in the Giants' gift to Gehrig on his retirement day, especially if the earlier slights were ultimately regretted.

Sadly, many of Gehrig's accomplishments were achieved in the shadow of other players or events, but he never complained. While he earned a right to mingle, at least metaphorically, with the greatest home-run hitters ever, for twelve of the seventeen seasons that he played professionally his accomplishments with the bat, especially hitting for power, were overshadowed by the man whom he had idolized as a youth and whom, despite their differences, he continued to believe was the greatest baseball player ever: Ruth. Gehrig accepted that. His career began ten years before the All-Star Game was initiated, and thus the total number of All-Star Game appearances he enjoyed was minimal compared with lesser players who came along later—he was only named to the American League squad seven times, but it would have been more had his career begun a decade later or his health remained intact. It didn't matter. Even his spectacular tryout with McGraw's Giants was overshadowed by the misfortune of a seeing-eye ground ball that found its way between his sturdy legs. With age comes wisdom, and he likely forgave McGraw. Finally, even the announcement of McGraw's retirement in 1932 overshadowed the greatest game of Gehrig's career, a game that most players only aspire to achieve. Few—only eighteen players in nearly a century and a half of baseball—have hit four home runs in a single game.

Through their personal and professional interactions with Gehrig, including several head-to-head World Series competitions, the Giants recognized that greatness had been in their midst all along. With Gehrig's retirement ceremony, they also realized that everything Gehrig had stood for and accomplished both in his life and on the ball field would soon come to a sudden, screeching halt. Gehrig, they understood, was one of a kind, and one-of-a-kind players only come along once in a great while. When they're gone, history is written, and the book is closed.

A fruit bowl and candlesticks seem inconsequential gifts in the context of a brilliant career that's about to end and a life that's flickering dimly. For Gehrig, however, the gesture counted for everything. The gift, perhaps a token of apology emanating from nothing more than McGraw's long-ago criticism of Gehrig and his subsequent decision not to offer him a contract or perhaps a nod of acknowledgment for the slugger's three World Series titles at the Giants' expense, was vindication enough—enough, in the end, to smooth things over and earn the "other" New York baseball organization some measure of recognition in the greatest sports speech ever presented.

"McGraw had . . . frightened [Gehrig] when he was a kid just off the Columbia campus," wrote the journalist Frank Graham of the Polo Grounds tryout. "But he had got to know McGraw in later years—to know him and to like him. And more than once, McGraw, looking at him and smiling, then shaking his head, had said: 'I wish I had paid more attention to you when you were on the Polo Grounds.' "[4]

Perhaps the gift reflected that sentiment. And although McGraw had died several years earlier, his love and appreciation for the man he refused to sign and in fact belittled as a college lad seventeen years earlier presumably trickled down to Gehrig and Eleanor in the form of a gift presented by Bill Terry and the entire Giants family. It's fair to assume that Terry, knowing the origin of Gehrig and McGraw's unusual relationship, ordered the gift as a proxy gesture on behalf of the deceased Hall of Fame manager—a gesture Gehrig couldn't fail to acknowledge on his final day as a Yankee player.

CHAPTER 11

THE YANKEES FAMILY

> Newspapers have said nice things about me, which I found hard to believe myself. . . . When the groundskeepers and office staff and writers and old timers and players and those boys in white coats all remember you with trophies, that's something.
>
> —Lou Gehrig, "Luckiest Man" speech

The little guy. Considering the enormity of his career, it's hard to believe that Lou Gehrig was once a little guy himself, a young man who hailed from the other side of the tracks, a high school kid from a low-income family who as a youth simply wanted to become an engineer. A little guy like the groundskeepers, office staff, writers, old timers, players, and concessionaires he spoke of. Once grown and out of his blue-collar neighborhood, he never gave himself too much credit for having risen above the lot he was given early on in life and for making something of himself. Despite his own success, however, Gehrig always remembered the little guy, and he treated those who were less fortunate than he was with compassion and respect. He wasn't a critical person, he wasn't demeaning, he never belittled. Instead, he went about the business of baseball in a dexterous manner, always performing up to his capabilities and never looking down upon people who were willing to work like he did in order to succeed in their chosen field.

Like groundskeepers. Following the Yankees' 1928 World Series sweep of the St. Louis Cardinals, Gehrig paid a visit to a friend in the Bronx who worked as a groundskeeper at the Yankees' home ballpark.

And concessionaires, those "*boys in white coats*." The team's official concessionaire honored the slugger with a special gift on Lou Gehrig Appreciation Day.

And writers. Gehrig had several close friends who were writers, including Fred Lieb—who cosponsored and invited Gehrig on a barnstorming tour of Japan—and John Kieran of the vaunted *New York Times*. On Lou Gehrig Appreciation Day, many of the "little people" flanked him as they stood like statues around the infield at Yankee Stadium. Gehrig doubtless appreciated their company on such a special occasion. They most certainly appreciated his.

Once he became a successful ballplayer, Gehrig interacted with the "little guys" he encountered as often as possible, from time to time playing baseball in the streets of New York with children from his own neighborhood. He was not above spending early summer evenings with wide-eyed young baseball enthusiasts, even after competing in long and exhausting games with the Yankees, nights when he was fully spent from battling the Red Sox or Senators or some other team and could use some rest or perhaps some family time alone with Eleanor. During an encounter with police after a neighbor complained about the racket that he and the children playing with him were making as they hit baseballs and circled makeshift bases, Gehrig was pleasant, courteous, and even lighthearted to the lieutenant who failed to recognize his famous visage at the station, pledging that from then on the boys would play their baseball at nearby parks and schools and he would confine his own exploits to Yankee Stadium. He left the police station having won over another little guy—this time a police lieutenant—as a new friend.

Closer to home were the writers, with whom Gehrig interacted often up until the end of his life. Compared with him, they were little guys, too. And while his relationship with the Fourth Estate was far from perfect, it was better than most ballplayers expected or experienced. As a result, he acknowledged them, along with the Yankees office staff, the "*old-timers*," "*those boys in white coats*" (the concessionaires), and others in his "Luckiest Man" speech. One such person was the renowned sportswriter Grantland Rice, with whom Gehrig fished and likely played cards while on the road.

Just weeks after Gehrig delivered his famous speech, Rice accompanied him, Bill Dickey, and Bucky Harris, longtime manager of the Senators, on a deep-sea fishing trip to a spot off the Maryland coast. During the trio's seafaring expedition, Rice, ever the inquiring journalist, used the

The Yankees Family | 103

Figure 11.1. Sportswriter Grantland Rice, 1920. Library of Congress.

restive occasion to interview Gehrig for an article that would appear in the *Hartford Courant* in August 1939. The slugger was in high spirits that day despite the perilous medical mountain that loomed in front of him, forcing him into the uphill battle of his life. He was happy to be out and about enjoying the mid-Atlantic sun and surf but happier to finally know with certainty just what he was fighting. As with baseball, as long as he knew the score Gehrig could aspire to victory, be it on the diamond or in the game of life. He was a consummate competitor.

"I knew something was far wrong," Gehrig told Rice between casts from the boat. "But I had no idea what it was. Even when I met the ball squarely [I felt] a child could have hit it harder. You can face any foe when you know who he is—even an incurable disease—but the other was different. The point is that the fog has lifted. I can now see the track up ahead, which is far better, even if it isn't the track I would have picked out."[1]

Later, on March 30, 1949, eight years after Gehrig's death, Rice sent a check to his widow as a contribution to the Lou Gehrig Memorial Fund. For some unknown reason, Eleanor had earlier contacted Rice with regard to the fund, and in response he enclosed a note of encouragement along with his contribution. Rice's typed note and Eleanor's response on the reverse side are historical artifacts. Rice wrote, "Dear Eleanor, I wish I could help more but will try to do better a little later on. This is a wonderful fund and certainly needs support." The note, showing that by then the two were on a first-name basis, is signed, "Sincerely, Grant,"[2] the familiar abbreviation for Grantland.

Eleanor responded to Rice's thoughtfulness with a brief, incomplete, scratched-out note, one apparently intended to assure her friend that she was not soliciting money when she contacted him earlier, contact that seems to have elicited his donation. Eleanor clearly did not wish to compromise the friendship by whatever it was she had written to her and Gehrig's longtime friend. The note was apparently never sent.

It was not unlike Gehrig to spend time with writers. When the Yankees were traveling from town to town, he and Dickey often played bridge and other card games with sportswriters who covered the team as a means of passing time. While it gave them something to do on long and exhausting road trips, the camaraderie they developed over such lengthy periods probably served another purpose, although it may not have been something Gehrig solicited: the relationships that developed between sportswriters and him may have produced increasingly positive coverage on the sports pages of newspapers that his card-playing adversaries represented. Among the participants in those late-night diversions were Rice, Kieran, and Lieb, each of them a well-known New York City scribe and each of them friendly with the Yankees player.

"Lou lives by copy-book maxims," the admiring Kieran once wrote of his clean-living neighbor and friend. "He has all the sturdy virtues. He doesn't drink. He goes to bed early. He is straightforward and upstanding."[3]

During the last decade of his life, Gehrig must have appreciated the writers who had collectively helped the Yankees land Joe McCarthy, who became a father figure of his, as manager following Huggins's death. They included *New York Sun* sports editor Joe Vila and sportswriter and Vila subaltern John Foster as well as *Chicago Herald-Examiner* sports editor Warren Brown, who combined their efforts, probably in collusion, to contact Yankees owner Jacob Ruppert and the team's general manager, Ed Barrow, to advise them that McCarthy was available and urge that McCarthy pursue the position. McCarthy did just that, and the decision the Yankees made to hire him as their next skipper had a significant impact on the remainder of Gehrig's career. He must have valued those scribes, whose efforts paid big dividends both for the organization and for Gehrig as his career moved into high gear during the 1930s.

While lesser known than the legendary Rice, Kieran, writing for the *New York Times*, was himself a noted journalist when Gehrig was playing for the Yankees. It was Kieran, a great admirer of the slugger, who was asked by the Yankees players to write the poem that was ultimately inscribed on the trophy presented to Gehrig by his teammates on Lou Gehrig Appreciation Day, a trophy the big first baseman cherished through his darkest days with ALS.

Those dark days didn't change the man; they only strengthened him. Gehrig remained modest and grateful. "In his speech, Gehrig didn't want to talk about himself—he talked about his teammates," said the former Yankee hurler Gil Patterson. "I was struck by his positive attitude and thankfulness. It seemed like in his speech he really appreciated everything God had given him, rather than ask, 'Why did God do this to me?' That speaks volumes."[4]

Lieb, a contributor to the so-called golden age of sportswriting in New York City, was also a friend of Gehrig. Like the better-known Rice, Lieb carved a niche in Gehrig's busy life and was one of the few people connected with baseball—Dickey was another—who attended Gehrig's Long Island wedding reception at the behest of the Yankee first baseman. So close were the two that in addition to inviting Lieb to attend, Gehrig also asked him to persuade Gehrig's own mother to attend the wedding, even though she didn't always get along with the slugger's future wife. Lieb, whose long career included stints writing for *Baseball Magazine*, the *Philadelphia News*, the *Sporting News*, and the *Baseball Research Journal*, complied with that request, and Mom Gehrig did attend the reception—to her son's delight. Lieb, whose wife, Mary, was especially close to Gehrig, may have known in advance that would happen—he was an avid devotee of Ouija boards.

It was Lieb who expressed concern for his close friend shortly after Gehrig became ill. When he overheard Eleanor describe her husband's chances of survival as fifty–fifty, he telephoned his personal physician to inquire about the disease known as ALS. Later, as Eleanor awaited definitive word on Gehrig's diagnosis, she asked Lieb to remain at their home until her husband telephoned her with the news from Minnesota, where the Mayo Clinic is located. He was happy to do so.

While Rice is among the best known of the journalists befriended by Gehrig, Kieran is remembered with greater emotion in the context of the famed Yankees' circle of writer friends, primarily due to his poetic contribution to Gehrig's retirement trophy. Although Kieran did an admirable job creating the verses, and his creativity was likely a labor of love, Rice was the confirmed poet of the group and wrote thousands of rhymes over his half-century career, many intermingled with his serious sports prose. Still, Kieran was given the assignment, and he came through in glorifying fashion. So adept was the writer at capturing the essence of Gehrig that the trophy now rests on display in the National Baseball Hall of Fame and Museum in Cooperstown, New York.

The Gehrig-Kieran friendship is a curious one. Now considered a legendary baseball writer more than forty years after his death in 1981, John Francis Kieran, born on August 2, 1892, in West Bronx, New York City, was eleven years older than the Iron Horse. Still, they related well to each other, and Kieran and his wife, Alma, often visited the Gehrig home, where the writer would play his accordion or discuss sports and other topics.

Kieran's first job, in 1915, was with the *New York Times* covering golf; he moved over to the *New York Tribune* in 1922, working as a baseball writer under Rice. He then shifted to the *New York American*, then back to the *Times*, then over to the *New York Sun* in 1941—the same year that Gehrig died. Kieran ended his newspaper career as a columnist for the *Sun* in 1944, three years after his wife died and he suffered his own health crisis in the form of a heart attack, likely due in part to the stresses he encountered over a quarter century covering high-profile sporting events. Kieran is a member of an elite cadre of baseball writers from the first half of the 1900s that includes the likes of Rice, Ring Lardner, and Damon Runyon, each of them a widely acknowledged pioneer of twentieth-century sports journalism.

Sid Mercer, who at that time was dean of sportswriters among those who had covered the Yankees, also was undoubtedly acquainted with Gehrig prior to serving as emcee on Lou Gehrig Appreciation Day, at least from having interviewed him. Since he had covered the Yankees and because the team felt him credible, it is certain the Yankees chose Mercer to emcee the event based upon his familiarity with the player and the fact that the two got along well; the team would not have allowed as master of ceremonies someone Gehrig didn't relate well to. If Gehrig and Mercer weren't close before, their July 4, 1939, exchange on the ball field at Yankee Stadium gave Mercer a boost in public recognition and a connection with Gehrig that would last forever, if only because he ran the show that day, or at least the public portion of it. Most important, he was the one who turned the microphone over to the Yankee great after Gehrig changed his mind and reluctantly decided to address the crowd. Mercer's role as emcee was fitting: he had watched firsthand as Gehrig helped reinvigorate the Yankees franchise in the early 1920s, essentially creating a baseball empire.

"That was really the start of the Yankee dynasty," said Greg Cadaret, who pitched for the organization from 1989 to 1992, winning twenty-two games during that four-year period. "That made them the juggernauts that they were and got the tradition going. It became ingrained."[5]

As master of ceremonies, it was Mercer's job to manage the flow of the event and to introduce the handful of people who would speak: Mayor La Guardia, Postmaster Farley, the home-run king Ruth, and the manager McCarthy. As each spoke, Gehrig smiled and applauded politely, and he graciously accepted a hug from Babe Ruth that technically ended their estrangement, although the two did not grow appreciably closer after that.

Fittingly, it had been those sportswriters covering the team who suggested that something be done to honor Gehrig in the first place after the seriousness of his illness and his planned retirement became known. Several suggestions were offered—these included retiring his uniform number and holding a special ceremony at Yankee Stadium complete with gifts and speeches. Both of those occurred.

As Gehrig stood on the grass that day, struggling to hold back his tears, Mercer announced that the Yankee was too overcome with emotion and would not be speaking. He then thanked the crowd for coming out to honor the man. Unfortunately for their quiet hero, those in the crowd would not be dismissed lightly, and they quickly and collectively took over, rising to their feet and chanting his name over and over. Finally, McCarthy, a father figure to the slugger, put his hand on Gehrig's back and gently ushered him over to the microphone, urging him to speak. Suddenly,

108 | Bronx Epitaph

Figure 11.2. Postmaster General James A. Farley, shown in 1937, was among those who spoke on Lou Gehrig Appreciation Day. Library of Congress, Harris & Ewing Collection.

Mercer's suggestion that Gehrig would not speak became irrelevant and his job that afternoon as master of ceremonies was complete—after Gehrig addressed the crowd there was nothing left for Mercer or anyone else to say or do. With his role as emcee completed, Mercer returned to his desk at the *New York American*; he would die six years later in 1945—just four years after Gehrig. Lou Gehrig Appreciation Day was over, and in time Mercer became one of the best-known masters of ceremonies in baseball history. Gehrig became a hero that day; however, it was Mercer who orchestrated the ceremony, strayed from the script, and permitted the Iron Horse to change his mind and speak without advance notice. An unbending writer might not have been so cooperative.

The "old timers" Gehrig referred to were represented by none other than Ruth, although he and Gehrig were estranged on the evening before Lou Gehrig Appreciation Day. That's when the first baseman began to outline his thoughts on paper in the event he was asked to address the crowd the following day. Exactly what transpired to force a wedge between the two stars is not known. Some say the disparity between their personalities created the chasm—Ruth was fun loving and boisterous, and Gehrig was shy and retiring—while others attribute their separation to alleged criticisms of Ruth's second wife, Claire, from Gehrig's mother.

Things apparently came to a head when the Babe spoke critically of his teammate's consecutive games streak, calling it an irrelevant statistic. "This Iron Horse stuff is just a lot of baloney," Ruth said. "I think he's making one of the worst mistakes a player can make. He ought to learn to sit on the bench and rest. They're not going to pay off on how many games he's played in a row."[6]

The separation was never resolved, except for a brief moment when Ruth, arriving late at Yankee Stadium for Lou Gehrig Appreciation Day, made his way onto the field, gave his own short address to the cheering crowd, then bear-hugged Gehrig prior to his teammate's "Luckiest Man" speech. With the crowd cheering, it appeared the two superstars had finally patched up their differences.

Meanwhile, the *old-timers*, as Gehrig called them in his speech, were on the field in all their splendor, lined up seemingly at attention along the Yankee Stadium infield. Ruth, long retired but already considered the greatest baseball player ever, led the pack of mostly former players. There were Tony Lazzeri, a future Hall of Famer and member of the organization's notorious Murderers' Row, and Hall of Famers Waite Hoyt, Earle Combs, and Herb Pennock, all of whom played with Gehrig on that brilliant 1927 team. Among such notable ballplayers, Ruth still symbolized the old-timers that Gehrig mentioned in his speech. Many of them dropped by to visit him in the Yankees clubhouse just prior to the game, reminiscing to the extent that at one point Gehrig exited the room with emotion etched

Figure 11.3. Herb Pennock loosens up in 1913 as a member of the Philadelphia Athletics a decade before he would join the Yankees along with Lou Gehrig. Library of Congress, George Grantham Bain Collection.

on his face before returning later to apologize to his mates for disrupting their fun. The sadness of the event was beginning to take its toll on him.

Not forgotten is Gehrig's thoughtful recognition of the Yankee Stadium concessionaires, headed by Harry M. Stevens, the purported mastermind of the hot dog and a distinguished caterer, who died in 1934 and left a treasure chest of valuable sports memorabilia to his heirs. Included was a letter written by Gehrig to the Stevens family after they presented him with a silver pitcher on his special day. Obviously, the gift meant a lot to Gehrig, and he said as much in his touching thank-you note to the company, dated July 7, 1939—three days after he received it: "Dear Stevens, I am still too overwhelmed and grateful to you fellows to be articulate, but I cannot wait longer to tell you how much I appreciated the silver pitcher and how valuable it is to me. It occupies a place of honor in my home, and I have the inscription facing the room to show anyone who visits me that three of the greatest fellows in the world are personal friends of mine."[7]

On Gehrig's special day, it was apparent the guard was changing. Concessionaire Stevens had died, and whenever a high-profile business owner dies things naturally change. It is likely that Stevens's passing resulted in some noticeable changes both within his company and at the ballpark.

The likable Ruppert also was gone, having succumbed to phlebitis and a liver ailment just six months earlier. His passing, which devastated the club emotionally, left the indomitable Barrow as team president.

Now, team captain Gehrig was preparing to depart the game of baseball just four years after Ruth had retired, leaving another monumental hole in the Yankees lineup, but one they would quickly close. By July 4, 1939, the vacuum created by Gehrig's retirement had been filled by the journeyman Babe Dahlgren, who stood near Gehrig that day in the event that he fell, and the Yankees were chugging along toward another world championship, this time sweeping the Cincinnati Reds in four games.

As Gehrig bid farewell to those who lined the infield, it must have gratified him to be honored by those he loved—from the big guys (McCarthy and general manager Barrow) to the little guys (the concessionaires, the writers, and the groundskeepers).

"*When the groundskeepers and office staff and writers and old timers and players and those boys in white coats all remember you with trophies, that's something*," he told his 62,000 listeners in a speech that touched the former Yankee Cadaret. "I think he was really appreciative of the opportunity he had had, the opportunity to make a living playing that game and the life that he had [as a result]," Cadaret said of the sheer thankfulness the slugger professed.[8]

As a light breeze blew across the ball field, it was only fitting that Gehrig mention those he did in his famous speech. Then, he stepped away from the microphones and disappeared into the Yankees dugout. Lou Gehrig would never play baseball again.

CHAPTER 12

MOTHER-IN-LAW

> When you have a mother-in-law who takes sides with you in squabbles against her own daughter—that's really something.
>
> —Lou Gehrig, "Luckiest Man" speech

Of all the people acknowledged by Gehrig in his farewell speech—which included the team owner Jacob Ruppert, the general manager Ed Barrow, the late Yankees manager Miller Huggins, then manager Joe McCarthy, and his parents, Heinrich and Christina Gehrig—one stands out. Relationships between married men and their mothers-in-law can be tricky at best, and many men veer away from discussing theirs in public, preferring to remain silent rather than inspire any conversation that could possibly turn contentious, as conversations about these relationships sometimes do. Gehrig was different from other men, however, and he let the world know it, describing Eleanor's mother, Nellie Mulvaney Twitchell, as someone who at times sided with him *"in squabbles against her own daughter."*

What made Gehrig's public exclamation even more unusual was that nothing was said in his speech about Eleanor's father, Frank Twitchell, who may have been estranged from the family by the time Gehrig entered the picture and married the Twitchells' daughter. Only Mrs. Twitchell was mentioned in Gehrig's speech, although not by name. It's not surprising that Mr. Twitchell was ignored. The couple eventually split up, and Mr. Twitchell apparently became separated from his family sometime during the late 1920s, only a few years before his apparent death in 1934. His omission from Gehrig's speech was understandable, as Twitchell was only conversationally a part of the slugger's life.

Nellie M. Mulvaney, born on March 17, 1884, was of Canadian and Irish descent. Her forebears entered the United States by ship during the influx of Irish immigrants that occurred after that country's devastating 1848 potato famine. While her husband claimed to be descended from Massachusetts gentry, Mulvaney one-upped him by claiming her own upscale lineage: that a king occupied her pedigree, although just which king is a mystery.

The redheaded Mulvaney, who as an adult was a small woman, was reared in a convent and lived at times with various cousins around the Chicago area. She and Twitchell met at a local horse-race venue and immediately were smitten, eventually marrying when Mulvaney was just seventeen. Their daughter recounted that Twitchell was the love of her mother's life, even after he exited the family scene for good around 1930.

Both Mulvaney and Twitchell emerged from Catholic backgrounds, although Mulvaney's religiosity was more concentrated. Her early life involved an immersion in the Catholic faith from morning until evening while living at the convent. The fact that the couple were drawn together is not surprising—he was so handsome that as a married woman Mrs. Twitchell would take her daughter to movies featuring Tyrone Power, whom she considered her husband's doppelganger.

The Twitchells' early years were rough and tumble, as the couple lived a peripatetic life; however, they eventually settled in at Sixty-First Street and Ingleside Avenue in Chicago, and Frank Twitchell began working as a racetrack pricemaker. Five years after Eleanor was born, her mother became pregnant again, this time giving birth to a son, Frank Twitchell Jr., in 1910. He died in 1975.

When Twitchell was hired to manage a well-known Chicago café, his wife felt a deep sense of pride in the appointment. There was also pride when Eleanor graduated from grammar school. Rather than force her daughter to make her own skirt and blouse for the ceremony, as was required of all female graduates, her mother completed the job herself.

Things eventually became tenuous between the couple, and Mrs. Twitchell visited an attorney for a divorce consultation. While there's no indication that she ever filed the necessary papers, she did learn to drive an automobile, which gave her a sense of independence as the marriage declined. A new freedom was emerging for Nell Twitchell.

Figure 12.1. Lou Gehrig (*left*) and Babe Ruth (*right*), 1931. Gehrig was the luckiest man for, among other things, having spent a decade playing alongside Babe Ruth, considered by many to be the greatest player ever. National Portrait Gallery, Smithsonian Institution.

It's not certain how Mrs. Twitchell survived after her husband disappeared—he is listed as head of the household in the 1920 census but not in 1930—however, her children, Eleanor and Frank Jr., apparently did what they could to help subsidize the family's well-being. With their various work situations, the two contributed enough to ensure the family's subsistence, including income from Eleanor's jobs with Saks Fifth Avenue and the Chicago World's Fair.

After Frank Twitchell Sr. left, Eleanor's marriage to Gehrig created a logistical problem for Mrs. Twitchell, as she wanted to live near to her daughter while the Gehrigs' new life unfolded. At about the time of her daughter's marriage, she used her modest savings to rent an apartment in the Bronx, leaving her just thirty minutes from her daughter and son-in-law's residence.

Mrs. Twitchell's efforts to remain in close proximity to Eleanor in the absence of the family breadwinner won Gehrig's admiration, evidenced by the homage he paid her in his famous speech. It was a considerate move by the beloved Yankee player.

"He was a beloved player because of who he was, not just because of how he played," former Yankee Mike Buddie said. "What he spoke that day came from his heart. When the people who are on your heart are your mother-in-law and the ticket takers, that says a lot about your character."[1]

Her new apartment also left Mrs. Twitchell in closer proximity to Gehrig's mother, who did not initially take a fancy to her. At that time approaching the age of fifty, Mrs. Twitchell behaved more like a young woman, a sister to Eleanor, than a middle-aged matriarch. Her husband had departed, her daughter couldn't cook, and Mom Gehrig's first meal with Mrs. Twitchell was served at a restaurant rather than in the home of her future daughter-in-law's family.

Her move to New York was not Mrs. Twitchell's only sacrifice for her daughter. At about the time Gehrig became ill, she moved in with the couple, presumably to assist her son-in-law as he underwent treatment and the couple's household duties took a back seat; she later moved with them to New York City when Gehrig became a parole commissioner. And when Gehrig passed away in 1941, she, along with Gehrig's parents, was at his bedside.

Gehrig gradually weakened—"like a great clock winding down"[2]—and Eleanor remained beside her husband as death neared, Tara Krieger wrote. "He slipped away quietly, the night of June 2, 1941, surrounded by Eleanor, his parents, and his mother-in-law."[3]

Even Gehrig's last words reflected his love for the woman. Looking up from his bed, he exclaimed, "My three pals," referring to his wife, his mother-in-law, and a trusted doctor.

Gehrig certainly understood his mother-in-law's devotion to his wife and, eventually, to himself, and he made sure her contributions to his and Eleanor's well-being did not go unnoticed. In the end, her devotion to Gehrig remained steadfast. At his funeral, Mrs. Twitchell and her daughter, along with Eleanor's brother and Mom and Pop Gehrig, occupied seats nearest to the church altar. It was an honor that reflected their place of importance in Gehrig's life at the very end.

CHAPTER 13

MOM AND POP

> When you have a father and a mother who work all their lives so that you can have an education and build your body, it's a blessing.
>
> —Lou Gehrig, "Luckiest Man" speech

A wide range of people resided in Lou Gehrig's world, but none were more important than his parents, in particular his mother. She loved him dearly, sacrificed her own needs to ensure that he received the college education she wanted for him, later became a favorite of Yankee players who thrived on her exceptional Old World style of cooking, and became his most ardent devotee as he moved up the ladder of success on the Yankees playing field. She may have been, in fact, his biggest fan.

In contrast to Gehrig's mother, his father was a staunch fan of his son's participation in sports right from the beginning, encouraging the young boy to strengthen his muscles, tune his body, and enjoy the fruits of his burgeoning interest in football and baseball—at first, Gehrig apparently showed more talent on the football gridiron than on the baseball diamond. Those fruits were ripe for the picking early on, and it was only a matter of time before the harvest came in.

Study long and hard, implored his dedicated mother, who hoped her boy would someday hold down a white-collar job, perhaps becoming an architect. Play sports equally as hard and always work to the best of your ability, intoned his struggling father, who must have hoped that baseball, even though he didn't understand the game's intricacies, would take his son to places he and his wife had only dreamed about, cities like Paris,

London, Rome, Cairo, and Munich. And, of course, baseball venues, such as Pittsburgh, Boston, and Chicago.

Those contrasting attitudes may explain the difference between Heinrich's and Christina's treatment of their son after he became a successful ballplayer. Both attended nearly every home game, with Pop Gehrig often somewhat critical and Mom Gehrig just the opposite.

In Christina's mind, her son could do no wrong, an attitude that likely resulted from the loss of three children early in their marriage and her pledge that the couple's fourth child would receive every possible encouragement—verbal, financial, or otherwise.

For the moment, however, the couple faced a conundrum—should their only child focus his attention on his studies, should he play sports as often and as intensely as he could, or should he strive to achieve both a first-rate education and athletic prowess and let the chips fall where they may? From the beginning the boy had studied *and* played hard; however, his skills on the field became obvious to even the most casual observers during his late teen years and early twenties. During that period, he naturally concentrated more on baseball, which he truly loved, with an eye toward becoming a professional ballplayer—on most days, he played, and

Figure 13.1. The Columbia University football team, presumably with Lou Gehrig in the huddle, competes on campus at Baker Field in 1922, as seen in an aerial photograph. Library of Congress, Adams & Grace Company.

played, and played some more. Life for Gehrig, at least following his all-too-brief Columbia University days, was mostly baseball, most of the time.

No one could argue that either parent was right or wrong in how they encouraged success for their sturdily built, highly intelligent, and immaculately groomed son, as both had the young man's best interests in mind. It was his success in the classroom that was certainly instrumental in getting Gehrig into a heralded Ivy League college and also helped carry him through his first year there, when baseball and football played second fiddle to his classroom work, at least in theory, and there were challenging issues concerning his amateur status.

It was not long before baseball eventually supplanted his classroom work and in time created the comfortable life the young man wanted and the world eventually came to admire and respect. Gehrig's mother was a good parent to insist that her son strive to complete his college education in order to avoid the hard knocks her husband continued to experience.

However, young Louis did not complete it, and he failed to become an architect as she had hoped or an engineer as the young man had initially wanted—but Pop Gehrig was also correct to insist that their only living child be allowed to fulfill his love for competitive sports.

Their agreement to his participation in sports while achieving a college education aside, Christina and Heinrich Gehrig were vastly different characters in an early-twentieth-century New York that continually evolved around their seemingly invisible Yorkville niche. Christina was domineering, a large woman who spoke her mind loudly and proudly at any cost, something that may have led to her son's later estrangement from the man he admired greatly as a teen: the mythical Babe Ruth. In contrast, Heinrich was of a less substantial build, although still a formidable man, and comparatively quiet like his son. Christina worked tirelessly for friends, acquaintances, and strangers in their New York City neighborhood, cooking meals, cleaning homes, and taking in laundry to make ends meet. Heinrich, an often-unemployed metal worker, was prone to spending long hours socializing at the local tavern, probably due to the excessive free time he had on his hands.

Lou's eventual wife, Eleanor, who once described her father-in-law as having a propensity for doing the wrong thing, insisted he was not a drunk but rather a tavern socialite. "Pop Gehrig wasn't a drunk," she wrote in her colorful 1976 autobiography, an obvious response to speculation that Gehrig's father drank to excess:

He loved the saloon because it was his club, a place where he could meet his friends, play pinochle, jaw about the old country, and do it all in German without any patronizing or muttering remarks from the "American" workers on the job. He wasn't lazy, either, but there really wasn't much work in his trade and maybe the saloon became an escape from that reality, or from home—because while Christina would never dare to put it that way, she didn't leave much doubt that her husband was something of a failure.[1]

A failure, perhaps, but not a loser.

Lou Gehrig's father, Heinrich Gehrich (note the spelling), was born into poverty on March 12, 1867, in Adelsheim in northern Baden-Württemberg, Germany, a state situated east of the Rhine River near his home country's border with France and Switzerland. Heinrich's parents (Lou's paternal grandparents) were Johann Philipp Gehrich, a carpenter, and Sophia Johanna Pfeiffer. In October 1888, with America between significant wars, Heinrich left behind his home, parents, siblings, and probably most of his possessions and boldly emigrated to the country where dreams were coming true for people who were crossing its borders from around the globe: the United States. At times he must have wondered why.

Gehrich, a Lutheran and the third youngest of nine children, eventually became "Gehrig," and after arriving in the country he first lived in Chicago, the hometown of his son's future wife. In time he moved to the Yorkville area of New York, where he likely figured his prospects as a metal worker were better, and quietly settled in a neighborhood largely populated with his own people—mostly immigrants from Germany and Hungary. It was in the Big Apple where Heinrich, a man of modest means and limited potential, first met Christina, also a Lutheran, who was fourteen years younger than he but, at twenty, was ready to marry. The couple were married in 1901,[2] less than two years before their only surviving son was born. They were still speaking German in the home until the boy was almost five years old.

Christina Gehrig was born Anna Christina Fack (sometimes spelled Facke) in Wilster, Schleswig-Holstein, near Germany's border with Denmark, on January 16, 1882, and she emigrated to the United States in 1900, more than a decade after her future husband came to America. While history does not record how, somewhere along the way the paths of Heinrich and Christina crossed in New York City, and the couple were joined in matrimony on November 27, 1901, settling into a melting pot that was home to low-income families of primarily European and Jewish origin.

Things were difficult for the Gehrig family from the outset as they tried to carve out their own version of the American dream with few traditional marketable skills—other than Christina's well-honed domestic capabilities and her husband's undependable metal expertise. The couple had four children in somewhat rapid succession, including Anna Christina, who was named for her mother and who died at three months of age in 1902; Sophie Louise, who died at age one in 1906; one unnamed boy who died in infancy around 1904 or 1905; and the only one who survived beyond early childhood, Henry Louis Gehrig, born in 1903 in a hot, cramped, and dusty apartment on the Upper East Side of Manhattan. Weighing in at a robust fourteen pounds, Gehrig would become known throughout the world only a generation after his birth.

"He's the only big egg I have in my basket," Christina once said. "He's the only one of four who lived, so I want him to have the best."[3] Thus the tone of their relationship was set for the remainder of Gehrig's life.

After Gehrig was born, the family struggled to survive on earnings that likely amounted to roughly several hundred dollars per year, placing them near the poverty level. Although poor by nearly every measurable standard, they were rich in one important thing: love. That didn't pay the bills, however, and Heinrich was unable, or often too sick—he later became essentially incapacitated—to eke out a living, something that placed the family in difficult straits and contrasted starkly with his son's commitment to never miss a game. Fortunately, Christina, a strong-armed woman, was an excellent cook and homemaker who was adept at Old World culinary arts and able to create such luscious delicacies as pickled eels, roast goose, whole roast pig, and sauerbraten, and she earned an acceptable living; after her son became famous she packaged those delicacies and transported them to the Yankee Stadium clubhouse, eventually hosting Ruth, Joe Dugan, Tony Lazzeri, and others as they enjoyed food and drink—including her homemade beer—in her own home, all prepared by a woman whom most of the team loved and admired.

Although times were usually tough, young Lou was far from ignored by his father, a man who understood his responsibility to earn a living, whose word at home was law, and who frequently took the boy to local gymnasiums to familiarize him with the joys of exercise equipment and body building. One Christmas he gave the budding baseball legend a right-handed catcher's mitt, but even in encouraging his son's baseball prowess his generosity turned out to be slightly misplaced. The boy eventually became a left-handed first baseman, and the mitt likely was cast aside after minimal use by the appreciative boy. Lou Gehrig would never be a catcher, let alone right-handed.

Adding to the family's legion of woes was the anti-German sentiment that increased in tone as World War I floated on the horizon. Heinrich and Christina eventually took work at a Columbia University fraternity, Christina as a cook and Heinrich as a handyman. Young Lou, who also helped out at a local fraternity house, was often referred to as "Heinie," a shortened version of the name Heinrich that often is used pejoratively and might have derived from a derogatory German term implying "moron" or worse. Historians have theorized that criticism of his German heritage in the years prior to and during World War I, as well as his poverty, likely contributed to Gehrig's shyness later on, an introversion he never completely overcame but that certainly did not hold him back on the most memorable day of his life: the afternoon he delivered his famous retirement speech.

Gehrig's mother, the family's primary and perhaps reluctant breadwinner, was exceedingly strong both emotionally and physically, weighing in at a robust 220 pounds—the same as her son's playing weight during his career with the Yankees. At her insistence, her son completed most of his high school studies, a rare feat for young men of his modest social and economic status, but he apparently did not earn a diploma. With his superlative skills on the ball field, a decision to attend Columbia University seemed the next logical step, at least to his mother, although because he was completing his high school education through an extension program, and because he had foolishly played minor-league ball after his first year at Columbia, Gehrig was prohibited from playing on the college football and baseball teams his freshman year. However, a season playing football in the fall of 1922 and baseball in the spring of 1923 followed, wherein he hit well over .400 while pitching Columbia to six wins; then, it was on to the New York Yankees and nearly fourteen years of playing without missing a game.

Early in Gehrig's career, his father still didn't understand the game of baseball, and he certainly didn't understand why his son sat on the Yankees bench day after day. He believed his son was a paid slacker and wondered what kind of work the boy was involved in that allowed him to do nothing.

Years later, Christina may have unwittingly played a key role in prolonging her son's consecutive games streak—by then, he was no longer a "slacker." On May 9, 1932, Gehrig skipped a ball game to support his mother as she testified in a lawsuit brought against her following a car accident that injured a passenger in her car. At stake in the litigation was a forty-thousand-dollar claim against his mother, and Gehrig did not want his mother to face the court challenge without family support. As a result, on that date he went straight to the courthouse instead of to Yankee Stadium. Across town, the Yankees coincidentally postponed the game that day, citing threatening weather—even though no rain fell. Gehrig's streak was intact, Mrs. Gehrig presumably testified with her son close by, and life went on as usual at Yankee Stadium.

As Gehrig succeeded as a Yankees ballplayer, his parents faded into the background more and more. After signing his first contract with the team, he bought them a home in New Rochelle, and for the first time their financial woes were over; Mom Gehrig would never have to work again, and the family would never again suffer the indignity and profound inconvenience of poverty. Gehrig, however, would continue to suffer the frustrations of his mother's day-to-day influence on his life. That, unfortunately for him and his future wife, who clashed with her mother-in-law on occasion, would never completely end. The frustration that Eleanor felt was certainly mutual, as Christina Gehrig never truly warmed to the only daughter-in-law she would ever have.

That chill was either mitigated or exacerbated when Gehrig married Eleanor in 1933: his mother did not attend the ceremony, laying to rest the question of which woman in Gehrig's life—his mother or his wife—would be more influential. Clearly, Eleanor had supplanted Christina as the most important woman in Gehrig's orbit, and in time his mother appeared to accept that.

There was trouble the following season when Ruth's second wife, Claire, whom Christina Gehrig also did not like, paid her a visit along with Ruth's daughter from his first marriage, Dorothy, and Claire's daughter from a previous marriage. Christina, who had liked Ruth's first wife, Helen, criticized what she perceived as Dorothy's tomboyish attire compared with the stylish garb worn by Claire's biological daughter, and the Bambino hit the roof. The incident created a rift between the families, and indeed the relationship between Gehrig and Ruth never completely recovered.

Christina's influence even extended to her son's play on the ball field. During the 1927 season, after which Gehrig was named the American League MVP, his production declined during the waning weeks of the season as Christina battled a thyroid inflammation followed by eventual surgery and her son paid daily visits to the hospital. He hit only .275

with two home runs over the last three weeks of the season, failing to pass the two hundred mark in runs batted in as some believed he might. Gehrig finished the season with 173 RBI.

"I'm so worried about Mom that I can't see straight," Gehrig said, hinting that his mother's condition had diverted his concentration and may have led to his statistical malaise during the final weeks of the season.[4] It all worked out for the better, however. In the end his mother was removed from the critical list, her disconcerting health situation was reversed, she was discharged following a lengthy hospital stay, and Gehrig went on to hit .308 in a winning World Series bid. On top of that, he was named the top player in the American League. For Gehrig it was time to look forward to the 1928 season.

Christina also influenced her son's personal life. As close as a mother could be to her son, she tried to prevent him from becoming involved with characters of dubious integrity and eligible women, not necessarily in that order, and Gehrig grew to become uncomfortable around marriageable young ladies. The result was that he spent as much time as he could with his parents or by himself, fishing with his father or riding the Rye Beach roller coaster—alone—for long periods. Would the most eligible bachelor in New York state and possibly the entire country ever marry anyone? If Mom Gehrig had anything to say about it, the answer was a definitive no. In the absence of any other consuming activities, he concentrated on winning games for the Yankees.

Over the course of his life, Gehrig faced—and overcame—numerous significant challenges, some of them resulting from the strict nature of his loving parents, and others coming from sources outside the family sphere. His father was chronically unemployed and was critical of his son at times. His mother was a different kind of challenge: she was tempestuous; discouraged his relationships with women, some of whom he might have married; resented the woman he did marry; and helped to compromise one of the most important interpersonal associations her son would ever have: that with his onetime baseball idol and teammate, the indomitable slugger Babe Ruth.

His wife, Eleanor, emerged as a bright spot in a sea of calamity, eventually eclipsing the loneliness he had experienced as an adolescent and later as a young adult. But even she had shortcomings, at one point not allowing Gehrig's mother into their home and failing to convey to her dying husband the seriousness of his devastating condition even after it became publicly known.

In the end, family harmony prevailed, and when Gehrig took ill his parents rallied behind him as they always had. On his final day of life, as Gehrig was losing his struggle with ALS, Heinrich and Christina joined Eleanor; her mother, who by then was living in her daughter and son-in-law's home; and a doctor for a final visit before Gehrig slipped into unconsciousness; he died hours later in the presence of his family. Despite the many shortcomings of his strong-willed parents and the pain they inadvertently inflicted on the son they cared so deeply for, his love for them remained intact and resounded for all to hear in his touching farewell speech.

"*When you have a father and a mother who work all their lives so that you can have an education and build your body, it's a blessing,*" he told the crowd, one of many tributes tendered in perhaps his final public appearance as a Yankee. In the eyes of the Yankees faithful, who had watched that body perform for seventeen seasons, it was a blessing indeed.

CHAPTER 14

TOWER OF STRENGTH

> When you have a wonderful wife who has been a tower of strength show more courage than I ever dreamed existed—that's the finest thing I know.
>
> —Lou Gehrig, "Luckiest Man" speech

For eight years, Lou Gehrig was, as the title of his wife's autobiography suggests, her Luke, and from 1933 until his death in 1941 Eleanor remained the most important woman in his life. For most of his thirty-seven years—thirty, to be exact—Gehrig was also his mother's Luke and, some have suggested, a mama's boy. That all changed on September 29, 1933, when Gehrig married Eleanor at their home at 5 Circuit Road in New Rochelle, New York. On that day, Gehrig ceased living with his parents—most importantly his mother—for the first time in his life. Most observers probably figured that after three decades it was high time he found his own digs.

"I've got a girl," Gehrig would unequivocally boast to those who inquired about his status with women prior to the time he met high-society lass Eleanor. Then he would add, "My mother! She's the best girl in the world."[1]

In 1932, on the evening before game three of the World Series against the Chicago Cubs, Gehrig attended a small dinner party hosted by a friend of Eleanor's, Kitty Perry, daughter of the man who owned the *Hammond Times* newspaper. Also attending that night was the woman he would eventually marry, none other than Eleanor. There, the two met—actually, for probably the second time. According to some accounts, Gehrig and his future wife had met for the first time several years earlier when Eleanor sat across the table from the slugger during another swank dinner party. If that meeting did occur, the two likely exchanged glances, even cordial pleasantries, and perhaps some light conversation, but Gehrig's mother was supposedly seated next to him, and he probably focused most of his attention on her rather than on the stunning beauty seated little more than an arm's length from him. After all, at that moment he considered Mrs. Gehrig, the mother, and not future Mrs. Gehrig, the wife, "the only [girl] I want."[2]

In her memoirs, Eleanor remembered their initial meeting differently, writing that their first encounter actually occurred before a Yankees-White Sox game at Comiskey Park when she was with a friend and the two were introduced by the friend's husband. Whether the fog of time impeded her memory is not certain—in her autobiography, Eleanor actually noted her birth year incorrectly, so her recollection could be wrong. Whichever story is accurate, everything would change four years later when

Figure 14.1. Fullback Lou Gehrig at Columbia University, ca. 1922. *New York Daily News*.

fate brought the two of them together in Eleanor's hometown Chicago. Fittingly, the World Series was the backdrop for renewal of their alleged earlier meeting. This time the introduction would stick, and the two would eventually be joined together in nuptial bliss, although without the blessing of Gehrig's mother.

Eleanor would write forty-four years later,

> The only flaw in the script was that Lou Gehrig was the straightest guy around, with a midnight curfew of his own whenever the Yankees were traveling. I think we were falling slightly in love that night, but I was no match for his curfew. I even started to leave before he turned into a pumpkin or something, but he rose to the occasion by asking if he could show me home. He did, but I was still no match for his code of conduct. A block away, at the door of my apartment, he abruptly said good-night and disappeared into the dark.[3]

Like a wraith.

Not for long. The following week an unexpected package was delivered to her door, one that contained a diamond-cut crystal necklace courtesy of the ever-so-shy Gehrig, and Eleanor responded with a handwritten note thanking him for his thoughtfulness. Gehrig, who had little experience with women, responded like a veteran with a note of his own. Then Eleanor responded again, and the rest is matrimonial—and baseball—history. From there things would proceed as might be expected considering that a high-society girl from one side of the tracks was dating a famous baseball player from the other side, a man who abided by his own strict curfew without exception.

Still, "Maybe we were star-crossed lovers from the start," she wrote.[4]

~

Eleanor Grace Twitchell was born on March 6, 1904 (she remembers it as 1905), in Chicago, nearly half a continent away from where her future husband would one day rule the ball fields of the American League. Her parents, Frank Bradford Twitchell and Nellie Mulvaney Twitchell, were of Irish descent, and despite an ancestry that the patriarch claimed was traceable to the first governor of Massachusetts, the family was eventually left in poverty by the Great Depression. Despite her modest beginning,

Eleanor grew up a lively and fashionable "society girl," as the local newspaper implied whenever there was occasion to mention her name in the context of a social affair or other semi-extravaganza.

Eleanor described her parents as nomads who worked for her great-uncle Gene Austin, a pricemaker before computers established racetrack betting odds. Because her father was a favorite of his, her great-uncle gave the young man a job and kept the position in the family for as long as he wanted it.

Reared in an apartment on Chicago's South Side, Eleanor attended a public grammar school as a member of what she called the comfortable poor, which placed the family somewhere between what she called the working poor and the very rich.[5] After grammar school she attended Hyde Park High School and later Chicago Saint Xavier Academy High but was ultimately a disinterested student, probably because she found outside activities more appealing to her socialite nature. The Twitchells eventually moved to Chicago's South Shore along the city's southern lakefront, and it was there that the family's fortunes began to change for the better, primarily when Eleanor's smart, imaginative father was named one of three city parks commissioners. One of his first accomplishments as parks commissioner was to order custom hot dogs from the supplier, Oscar Meyer, and the result was swift and a little unexpected: consumers came to the parks in droves to eat at his food stands.

Other ingenuity followed: Twitchell refurbished several old buildings at a Jackson Park golf course, creating a significantly upgraded clubhouse. He also turned the aging German Pavilion, which was built for the 1893 Chicago World's Fair, into a bathing center. And he created a gazebo near the halfway point at the Jackson Park course, a structure where golfers could grab a bite to eat before beginning their final nine holes of play. To reward himself for his many efforts, Twitchell bought a Stearns-Knight luxury automobile and later a Franklin.

The pay that Twitchell earned from his various ventures was doubtless more than reasonable, and as a result Eleanor was exposed to many of the finer things in life, including riding, golf, and ice skating. As the young woman matured and gravitated away from her family, she was also exposed to some of the less fine things in life, becoming a regular poker player with her girlfriends and a patron of the local racetrack.

Unbeknownst to Eleanor, Gehrig, the man she would one day marry, was struggling with his own family in a poor section of New York. Those contrasts, which the Yankees contract helped him overcome, would play a role in the evolution of their successful marriage years later.

Things became harrowing at the Twitchell household when race riots broke out in Chicago in the summer of 1919, just before the start of the infamous World Series involving the Chicago White Sox, later to become known as the Black Sox. Twitchell, it seems, had been hiding local African American residents in the German Pavilion, protecting them from those who wanted to hang them. The notion that he might eventually be caught was nerve-racking to Eleanor; however, her father's good deeds were never discovered by antagonists. By 1930, her father had disappeared, and Nell was head of their household. By 1934, Frank Twitchell, apparently estranged from the family, was likely dead.

As a diversion, Eleanor began hanging out at Comiskey Park, home of the White Sox, with close friends, one of whom had access to her father's stadium box. If she ever saw a Yankees-White Sox game after Yankee Stadium opened in 1923, the same year that Gehrig signed his contract with the team, she certainly saw her future husband ply his potentially lucrative trade at one time or another. She probably didn't give the big first baseman a second thought.

During the Roaring Twenties, Eleanor, like many others in that decade of decadence, ratcheted up her extracurricular activities with friends, smoking and drinking while collecting big winnings at the racetrack. Through it all she continued to receive a modest allowance from her father, who may not have known he was helping to keep his daughter in cigarettes and liquor. However, while living the single life in all its splendor, Eleanor's secret goal was anything but to remain by herself. She wanted a wealthy husband, perhaps even a millionaire—something Gehrig was not.

Before she had a chance to fulfill that dream, misfortune struck. While golfing one day, she suffered a dizzy spell, and it alarmed her enough to see a doctor. What he told her was not something she wanted to hear: Eleanor had what the physician described as a heart leakage. No treatment was prescribed other than to cut back on her golf outings, ride horses less, and minimize her Charleston dance adventures.

Like anyone diagnosed with a potentially serious health problem, Eleanor sought an evaluation by a second doctor. The next one was far more lenient in his assessment, informing her that the condition was not in fact serious and recommending, among other things, that she spend less time golfing and avoid debilitating love affairs. At that time Eleanor had no such love affairs in tow.

By then, Eleanor's home life was deteriorating. To achieve some added independence as the marriage her parents had once enjoyed faltered, she sought employment at a new store in Manhattan called Saks Fifth

Avenue in March 1929 and was hired as secretary to the general manager. Seven months later, the stock market crashed, sending companies across the country into financial turmoil. Even the ostentatious Saks, where floor sales staff were required to wear carnations, was not exempt.

By the time the market crashed on Black Tuesday, 1929, Eleanor had risen to become the unofficial director of personnel for Saks, earning a hefty thirty dollars per week, and it was her job to hire new employees and fire expendable ones. One day a new manager arrived, and she found that her own number was up at long last. The manager, her fourth since joining the company, promptly fired her. "Miss Twitchell had been sacked by Saks," Eleanor wrote in her autobiography.[6]

Across town, where Yankees field boss Miller Huggins had died only a month earlier, Gehrig had a replacement manager of his own, Art Fletcher, who like his predecessor demanded nothing less than 100 percent effort from his players. Former pitcher Fred Kipp said the same expectation applied to players when he was with the club thirty years later in 1960: "Oh, yeah," he said, adding that the ambitious organization-wide expectation likely originated during the Gehrig-Ruth era. "[Gehrig] went to the post every day and I imagine he gave 100 percent every day. He was a big, strong guy."[7]

With the country in turmoil and people everywhere looking for employment, Eleanor wasn't out of a position for long. Within thirty minutes she was hired as a secretary with the Century of Progress planning committee for the 1933 Chicago World's Fair, for forty dollars per week. Out of a job only briefly, she had landed on her feet with energy and confidence. The Great Depression, which had left much of the nation reeling with despair, clearly wouldn't hold her back.

Then, with suddenness, along came Gehrig, whom Eleanor wrote about in a tune penned with songwriter and friend Fred Fisher, which was published two years after the Gehrigs' 1933 marriage. Titled "I Can't Get to First Base with You," the song was anything but memorable, except, perhaps, from a baseball perspective. Penned in 1935, it is probably the only love song ever written that intermingles sacrifice bunts, a trot to first base, winning, innings, and getting a hit in order to win a suitor's heart. Fortunately, Gehrig and Eleanor didn't have to go to all that trouble to win each other's affections. Incidentally, the songwriter Fisher stuck with his better-known song, "Peg o' My Heart," and the world was a better place for it. It is not known whether Eleanor ever again dabbled in musical interludes.

Of the different accounts of Gehrig's first meeting with his future wife, the baseball version is preferred. Like everyone else, she was familiar with the name Lou Gehrig. According to Eleanor, one day in 1928 she was visiting Chicago's Comiskey Park with friend Dorothy Grabiner. During the pregame activities, Grabiner's husband called Gehrig over to his wife's box near the Yankees dugout and introduced him to the young socialite. Gehrig tipped his cap, exclaimed that he was pleased to meet her, and promptly waltzed away. That was it . . . until 1932.

The get-together at friend Kitty Perry's apartment was informal, and Eleanor was excited to once again meet the famous baseball player. During the evening, his eyes remained frozen on her, and toward the witching hour he took her home. There was no kiss, no stolen moment on a porch swing, no promise of another meeting. The shy first baseman, who had dated some but had never really had a steady girlfriend, was not accustomed to the niceties of dating, and he vanished into the cool Chicago evening.

Surprisingly, he called her up the following week and presented his new friend with the infamous crystal necklace, which he'd bought overseas. Gehrig had lavished jewelry on his mother for many years, but his gift of a necklace to Eleanor may have marked the first time he ever gave such a prize to a lady friend.

The courtship blossomed, and eventually the couple were married—for better or for worse, as their vows likely promised. In time, the worse seemed to overshadow the better. First, there was Gehrig's mother, the hard-nosed Christina, who created problems for the couple from the get-go. Not used to playing second fiddle to any woman, the intransigent Christina held fast to the notion that her son belonged with his mother and not a wife. When the couple first announced to her that they would marry, she promptly announced to them that she would not attend. At Gehrig's request, the writer Fred Lieb was called in to mediate the situation, and he offered to drive Gehrig's mother to the wedding ceremony. Although Christina declined the invitation, Lieb informed the matriarch he would pick her up late in the afternoon on September 30 and that she should be ready.

The animosity between Eleanor and her future mother-in-law eventually boiled over, and the couple decided to marry privately on September 29, with the groom attired in shirtsleeves and the bride adorned in an apron. All about them, workers were scurrying for room as they hustled through the dusty mess to complete some needed improvements in the couple's new home. Gehrig then headed for Yankee Stadium and a game against the Washington Senators. While he was then 1 for 1 in marriage proposals, the new husband batted zero against the last-place Senators that day, going 0 for 4.

Incidentally, Lieb followed through on his good friend's request and picked up Gehrig's mother the next day promptly at 5:30 p.m.—to attend her son's wedding *reception* rather than the actual ceremony.

After the wedding, reality set in: Gehrig's mother resented his new wife and lived in fear that her son's financial and other support would eventually dry up. Of course, it didn't. Her loving son eventually created a trust for his parents that included his entire savings. His parents were awarded a monthly allowance that started at two hundred dollars and was payable for the rest of their lives as well as a new car and a deed to the couple's house in New Rochelle. The gifts would ensure that his parents, especially his mother, would live happily ever after.

Still, Eleanor remained the number-one woman in his life, as he hinted in his retirement speech at Yankee Stadium: "*When you have a wonderful wife who has been a tower of strength show more courage than I ever dreamed existed—that's the finest thing I know.*"

When the speech was over, his focus turned to defeating a killer disease, one that would rack his seemingly indestructible body for the remainder of his young life. Through it all, his wife would remain a *tower of strength*.

CHAPTER 15

AWFUL LOT TO LIVE FOR

> So I close in saying that I might've been given a bad break, but I've got an awful lot to live for. Thank you.
>
> —Lou Gehrig, "Luckiest Man" speech

When an ailing Lou Gehrig stepped back from the microphones and, at least symbolically, away from the field of play forever, he withdrew from a sport that gave his life purpose. Since winning big games for the High School of Commerce and later for Columbia University, Gehrig had played the game of baseball competitively for nearly a quarter century and had become a virtual household name. He had performed on the diamond with an abundance of skill and as a result was paid handsomely. Not as well as Babe Ruth, perhaps, but he wasn't the personality that Ruth was, and he hadn't the same star quality. Despite those shortcomings, if they were in fact shortcomings, Gehrig played well enough to buy his parents a nice home, support a wife whose tastes in clothing and other niceties were slightly on the extravagant side, and enjoy the many perks that highly paid athletes could afford: world travel, fine dining, and a nice home, among other things. Certainly, if Gehrig had been asked before he was diagnosed with ALS to list the many things he had *to live for*, baseball would have topped the list.

Gehrig always had *an awful lot to live for*. As a teen, he lived for the high school baseball championship in Chicago, where his late-inning grand slam elevated him to prep prominence. He later lived to try out with the New York Giants, eventually becoming a professional baseball player and winning the World Series—eight times, in fact. Finally, he lived to marry the only woman he ever really loved. All along the way, from grade school through high school and adulthood, Gehrig had *an awful lot to live for.*

As an adult Gehrig had baseball friendships *to live for* as well, including trusted confidant Bill Dickey, the manager Joe McCarthy, and even the vociferous and fun-loving Ruth early in his career, a bona fide star with whom he once had roomed during Yankees road trips and a player who colluded with him on a short-lived but popular barnstorming tour that spanned the entire length of the United States, starting in the east and finally closing out in sunny California.

After the Yankees' sweep in the 1927 World Series, Gehrig and Ruth were in great demand by fans across the country. To satisfy the public's insatiable interest in the slugging duo, Ruth's business representative came up with an ingenious plan: Why not let the public at large see the two stars up close in an entirely different environment than they were used to? With that in mind, he orchestrated a coast-to-coast baseball tour that allowed fans to get a closer look at their Yankee heroes as they performed alongside less-prominent local ballplayers. Gehrig would compete for a team called the Larrupin' Lous and Babe would play for the Bustin' Babes, their respective teams composed of players enlisted from the many local communities the sluggers would visit along the route that their unusual baseball demonstration was to take. During the tour they played games from the East Coast and mid-Atlantic regions through the heartland of America and on out to the Pacific Coast and Southern California, entertaining roughly 250,000 fans in more than one-third of all the US states. Tour venues included Brooklyn, New York; Asbury Park, New Jersey; Duluth, Minnesota; Kansas City, Missouri; Lima, Ohio; Omaha, Nebraska; Des Moines and Sioux City, Iowa; Denver, Colorado; and San Francisco, San Jose, Fresno, Marysville, Stockton, Santa Clara, Los Angeles, and San Diego, California. With friends like tour-mate Ruth, Gehrig must have believed he had *an awful lot to live for* in his personal relationships—at least until his much-celebrated spat with the Sultan of Swat broke things off and left them alienated.

Later, following his marriage to the gregarious Eleanor, Gehrig changed his tune somewhat, as his few close friendships at once took a back seat to his socially astute wife. What did Gehrig have *to live for* at that point? *An awful lot,* at least in the person of Eleanor, a beautiful woman who at last supplanted his mother as the most important woman in Gehrig's life.

Not that his parents, in particular his mother, didn't give him much *to live for* as well. By the time his play began to suffer, and his illness was discovered by clinically interrogating Mayo Clinic physicians following a week-long visit to the Rochester, Minnesota, hospital, Pop Gehrig was virtually incapacitated, unable to perform the daily rigors that a metal worker needed to perform. Mom Gehrig had grown apart from her daughter-in-law, and their relationship had become a significant drain on Gehrig's emotional health, although a lesser drain than the ALS would become on his physical health. By then, his parents had grown old: in 1939, Mom Gehrig was fifty-seven and her husband was seventy-two, he having far exceeded the projected life expectancy for a man at that time and she only a few years from exceeding the life expectancy for a woman. While Gehrig's parents still presented him with *an awful lot to live for*, other priorities were about to converge. They had to if Gehrig's life was to ever have meaning beyond baseball.

Finally, he had close friends in the media *to live for*, most notably the author and journalist John Kieran, who worked as a senior sports columnist for the *New York Times*. So close were Gehrig and Kieran that the writer may have stepped out of bounds for a journalist when he wrote his eulogistic poem that was fixed to the player's trophy Gehrig received from his teammates as he modestly offered his emotional resignation from baseball. Kieran continued to visit Gehrig long after he took ill, at times accompanied to his friend's home by his wife, Margaret, also a journalist.

Suffering with an incurable and debilitating disease, unable to ply his trade playing baseball, his friendship with the affable Ruth forever compromised by a possible verbal indiscretion, his parents getting along in age, and his wife the only realistic and truly meaningful diversion he had remaining (other than fishing), Gehrig needed something more to feel at least somewhat whole. At about that time, along came Mayor Fiorello La Guardia, a former two-time congressman and the ninety-ninth mayor of New York City. La Guardia was, it seemed, the least likely person to come alongside Gehrig in his hour of need. Perhaps that's what Gehrig needed most—a new interaction, a least likely friend rather than a tried-and-true teammate or newspaperman.

The two were a study in contrasts: at five feet, seven inches tall, the rotund La Guardia was quick-tempered and spirited, with a magnetic personality. In contrast, Gehrig, at an even six feet and by then perhaps 220 pounds and still outwardly physically fit, was shy, modest, and somewhat withdrawn. The only thing the two appeared to have in common was a

Figure 15.1. One of the things Lou Gehrig had to live for was his budding relationship with New York City mayor Fiorello La Guardia, seen leaving the White House in 1938, the year before the mayor appointed Gehrig to the New York City Board of Parole. Library of Congress, Harris & Ewing Collection.

love for the Yankees, as La Guardia had demonstrated when he addressed the crowd at Yankee Stadium on the day that Gehrig bid farewell to the team he had faithfully helped lead to numerous World Series titles over his sixteen years in professional baseball. La Guardia, it seemed, was a perfect ally at just the right time in Gehrig's life. A much-needed diversion was on the horizon.

Perhaps in 1939 Gehrig did have a *lot to live for* even without La Guardia. If that were true, he would have much more to live for with the mayor in his corner. La Guardia needed a commissioner for the New York City Board of Parole, and Gehrig needed a purpose in his diminishing life. With a simple phone call initiated by the mayor, each got what he wanted.

It all began on October 10, 1939, when the telephone rang at the Gehrigs' Larchmont home several days after his final World Series. The mayor was calling with an offer unrelated to the only thing Gehrig knew how to do: play baseball. After inquiring about Gehrig's future intentions following his recent retirement and receiving an uncertain response, La Guardia offered him a proposition. An opening for commissioner had arisen on the parole board, and the mayor believed Gehrig was the perfect person to fill the position. The icing on the cake was that the job afforded the slugger an opportunity to help young people who needed a break to get their lives back on track. Well aware that Gehrig had recently suffered his own *bad break* in life, La Guardia asked whether he might be interested in filling the position. Gehrig thought for a nanosecond, then responded affirmatively.

The two chatted about the position for some time. Then, as their conversation wound down, La Guardia told Gehrig that his salary would be a comparatively modest six thousand dollars per year, adding that he would prepare to announce his new appointment to the news media. Then, the two hung up, and the Gehrigs began laying the groundwork for a move to Riverdale in New York City, a requirement of Gehrig's new job. Eleanor's mother joined the couple in their new home.

Like her husband, Eleanor was also thrilled at the opportunity the mayor had given him. The new position would perhaps divert from his mind some of the lingering concerns he understandably had about his health, and she agreed with the mayor that as a parole board commissioner her husband would have ample opportunity to assist young adults who may have strayed from the law largely due to a lack of direction or guidance early on in their lives. What better person to get their attention than someone who had been getting people's attention as a baseball player for the better part of twenty-five years?

It wasn't only his background as a famous ballplayer that made Gehrig a suitable—indeed, ideal—candidate for the position. He had been born and reared in New York City, knew the neighborhoods well, had been in and out of mischief himself as a young boy consorting with friends, and had even known young men whose poor upbringings had landed them in trouble. La Guardia's offer presented Gehrig with an opportunity to take what he'd learned both in baseball and on the streets of New York City and put it to good use for the benefit of those less fortunate and the overall betterment of society. Sure, Gehrig had an incurable disease. Sure, there was no guarantee how long his health would permit the slugger to fulfill his commitment to La Guardia and the parole board. But Gehrig was game to give the position his best shot, and La Guardia wanted nothing more than to see what might transpire and for how long. Gehrig was grateful for the opportunity.

"I want you to know that you gained an admirer on the day of our meeting," Gehrig wrote in a letter to La Guardia. "It is heartwarming to receive the sympathy and plaudits of the crowd, but it is something more to receive a simple, honest, and unbiased offer such as you extended me."[1]

As a parole commissioner, Gehrig's duties were cut and dried: he would travel around New York from prison to prison, interview and advise those who were incarcerated, and ultimately recommend which prisoners ought to be freed and which should not. While the money he earned was far less than he was used to receiving as a ballplayer and his office was far from extravagant, Gehrig enjoyed doing something he considered significant, something that truly made a difference in the lives of the men he was charged with helping.

After La Guardia swore in Gehrig, the now-former ballplayer began his theoretical ten-year term as parole commissioner. The Gehrigs relocated to the Bronx, and Eleanor's mother quietly moved in with the couple—a testament to the depth of the relationship between Gehrig and his mother-in-law and how well the two got along. Then, it was down to business, with Gehrig driving himself to work each morning at 9:00 a.m. While there, he completed paperwork, visited prisons, interviewed prisoners, reviewed their records, and ultimately made decisions regarding their incarceration.

While Gehrig started off enthusiastically, it wasn't long before his depreciating condition began to cause him problems. While on the job he became fatigued easily, and his clothing at times appeared slightly disheveled. Because writing eventually became a chore for him, Gehrig signed papers using a signature stamp. Visitors to his office also noted that the former slugger sometimes held a telephone receiver awkwardly, probably because his fine motor skills were starting to decline. Finally, in the winter of 1939, Gehrig's physician urged him to stop working altogether. Initially, he did not. Then, he did.

After halting work at last, Gehrig's earlier claim of having an *awful lot to live for* had diminished considerably, or so it seemed. His once-perfect health was noticeably receding, he was barely employable, and the adulation he had once been accustomed to receiving was a thing of the seemingly distant past. Despite those considerable personal losses, losses that might shred a weaker person, Gehrig still had his loving wife, supportive parents, mother-in-law, and close friends to support him, cheer him on, and assist him during his physical decline, which they faithfully did.

In a sense, they reflected the indomitable spirit that remained alive when Yankees alum Mike Buddie was on the team and certainly remains alive within the Yankees organization today. "There was an underlying tone of a huge responsibility to uphold the pinstripes," Buddie said. "There was an expectation that was probably deep rooted in the type of person Lou Gehrig was, the understanding that if you're not going to hit four hundred home runs then you better uphold that level of integrity."[2]

If family and close friends are at all consequential to a desperately ill person's well-being, if they can hold any sway in life-and-death situations, then Gehrig still had *an awful lot to live for*. Unfortunately, his unrelenting disease, as it closed in on its once-vibrant host, had other ideas.

For Gehrig, time marched on—slowly at first, then quickly, relentlessly. The resounding cheers he had grown accustomed to hearing over seventeen high-profile baseball seasons were now silent, or at least redirected toward a new fan favorite: Joe DiMaggio. The joy Gehrig felt wearing Yankees pinstripes turned to profound sadness, then nothingness, his wool flannel pinstripe uniform replaced by single-button pinstripe suits, then finally pajamas. Gone were his mud-caked black cleats; a pair of shiny oxfords and later slippers instead covered his increasingly shuffling feet. Home to him was no longer Yankee Stadium; Gehrig instead resided full-time at his house in the Bronx. His teammates toward the end were his best friends: his parents, his wife, his doctors, and his beloved mother-in-law.

As it usually does with ALS, death also came slowly, then quickly, relentlessly. At some point Gehrig probably knew what his wife and general manager had tried to hide from him: that life, his life, was finite, and that it would end with a whimper, sooner rather than later. He eventually accepted that, content, as much as he could be, to sit at home with his wife. The days ticked by, then the weeks and the months.

At 10:00 a.m. on Monday, June 2, 1941, with Gehrig's health as bad as it could possibly get, Eleanor, her mother, and a doctor were gathered around Gehrig's bed as death encroached upon their home near the Henry Hudson Parkway. At one point the slugger looked up at the worried trio and exclaimed, "My three pals."[3] He then slipped into a coma that lasted throughout the day. Finally, the end came shortly after 10:00 p.m. Lou Gehrig, the Iron Horse, the ballplayer who would never die, who *could* never die, in fact did. His Bronx epitaph, presented on July 4, 1939, would be a lasting memorial, talked about for days, weeks, months, years, decades.

Of all those who might have been summoned to the Gehrig home initially—best friend and teammate Dickey among them—it was general manager Ed Barrow and his wife who were among the first to be notified, called by the family as Gehrig appeared to be slipping away; he raced through town to get there. The Barrows arrived at the late slugger's home before anyone else, followed next by Ruth and his wife, Claire, both of whom were in tears; no one else paid their respects until the following morning, when news of Gehrig's death began to spread. The fact that Barrow was the first to arrive at the Gehrig residence is a tribute to his and the player's long-standing friendship—despite the salary disagreements that punctuated Gehrig's seventeen-year tenure with the Yankees club.

More than a baseball team, the Yankees considered themselves a family, and the organization had just lost a member of that vaunted family—*baseball's greatest empire*, as Gehrig described it in praising Barrow during his "Luckiest Man" speech. The description and praise were well placed, blazing a legacy for the Yankees' chief architect during the team's rise to greatness that far exceeded his earlier legacy of converting Babe Ruth to a home-run hitter. That legacy continued long after Barrow's and Gehrig's deaths—and in fact continues today.

"When I heard stories about Lou Gehrig and that speech, I could tell that it was so engraved in the history of the New York Yankees that I really felt proud to be part of that organization," said former Yankee Rick Dempsey, whose tenure with the team occurred early in his career and who ultimately played twenty-four seasons in the major leagues. "Lou Gehrig epitomized everything about the Yankees and what they meant to the game of baseball."[4]

More than eighty years later, Gehrig's words continue to echo: *Today I consider myself the luckiest man on the face of the earth*. Perhaps that was true then; would that it were. Most would agree that there appeared to be little good luck at the end of Gehrig's life, only bad. Death from a degenerative disease is never easy, never lucky.

If there's one takeaway from Lou Gehrig's life, it is this: luck is in the eye of the beholder. Standing before 62,000 teary-eyed admirers, with death knocking at his door, Gehrig proclaimed himself *the luckiest* of the lucky. Who's to argue with that? Who's to know a man's personal standard for good luck, and who's to object when he reveals it? In the end all a man has are the blessings he has accumulated in his life, the good things he holds dear. Some call that luck. Gehrig did. Was Gehrig *the luckiest man on the face of the earth*, or the unluckiest man simply trying his hardest to keep up a bold front? Truth be told, Gehrig was probably the former, a very lucky man, even at the end. The luckiest. After all, in death as in life, it's hard to argue with Lou Gehrig.

EPILOGUE

> As long as I was following Babe to the plate I could have gone up there and stood on my head. No one would have noticed the difference. When the Babe was through swinging, whether he hit one or fanned, nobody paid any attention to the next hitter.
>
> —Lou Gehrig

Eight decades after Lou Gehrig's death, the names of his mentors roll from the tongue as a who's who of New York Yankees lore: Miller Huggins, his first manager. Joe McCarthy, his last manager. Jacob Ruppert, the team owner. Ed Barrow, general manager and later president of the Yankees. Gehrig's few family members, each of them noted in his famous speech, although none by name, are added to the mix: his wife of fewer than six years, Eleanor, and his parents, Heinrich and Christina Gehrig. Finally, there was Eleanor's mother, Nellie Twitchell, Gehrig's mother-in-law. If there ever was an unusual concoction of thank-yous and kudos bestowed during a high-profile public event, this was it. As the guest of honor, however, Gehrig made the acknowledgments work, leaving no one out. Well, maybe one person.

Eighty years later it remains unclear whether Gehrig mentioned the larger-than-life figure Babe Ruth. Only sportswriter Shirley Povich hinted at it in an article that appeared in the *Washington Post* later that day. Wrote Povich, "He didn't forget [to mention] the late Miller Huggins, or his six years with him; or manager Joe McCarthy, or the late Col. [Jacob] Ruppert, or Babe Ruth, or 'my roommate, Bill Dickey.'"[1] Babe Ruth?

Indeed, Povich, who erred in transcribing Gehrig's exclamation "I've got an awful lot to live for" to instead read "I've lots to live for, honest,"[2] may also have erred in recollecting a Ruth reference, or perhaps he was referring to the hug the two shared on the field or some other mention of his name during the proceedings—Gehrig and Ruth had not been close for several years, and any mention of the Babe would have been surprising. It also would have been covered by other reporters; however, research indicates otherwise. Certainly, people might have thought the sluggers were close, and often they were identified like bosom buddies: Ruth and Gehrig, people would say. Gehrig and Ruth. Like Tom and Jerry, Mutt and Jeff, peanut butter and jelly. In reality, the two were more like Lincoln and Douglas. However, for the last several years of their careers, Ruth and Gehrig, Gehrig and Ruth, didn't speak to each other, a standoff that would end on that breezy afternoon in Yankee Stadium, known affectionately as the House That Ruth Built—Babe Ruth.

"I was surprised that in his speech Gehrig didn't mention Babe Ruth," said former Yankee Gil Patterson. "He didn't talk about the Babe."[3] Or did he?

In the Yankees' day-to-day lineup, where Ruth's name usually appeared there was always Gehrig.

For twelve long, memorable, and highly productive seasons as members of the team's legendary Murderers' Row, the duo filled the number three (Ruth) and four (Gehrig) spots in the batting order almost every game, and they usually did so quite effectively—they homered in the same inning nineteen times, in the same game seventy-two times, and for more than a decade they attracted high-profile media attention almost daily. The pair even committed some adolescent shenanigans on occasion, mostly when they were younger and there wasn't silence to separate them. Despite all of that, Ruth and Gehrig were really quite different—the Babe with his high living, Gehrig with his shy reticence. They respected each other's ability to hit baseballs and to help their team win ball games, but beyond that they generally went their separate ways when not on the playing field. It was hot dogs and beer for the twice-married Ruth, who usually spoke his mind more freely and decisively than some people wanted, and quiet home cooking for Gehrig, away from the pressing throngs and instead relaxing with the love of his life, Eleanor.

∽

Babe Ruth was born George Herman Ruth in Baltimore, Maryland, on February 6, 1895, one of eight offspring of George Sr. and Kate Ruth.

Figure E.1. Babe Ruth shortly before the franchise-changing deal that sent him to the Yankees in 1920. Library of Congress, National Photo Company Collection.

From the beginning of his life, in a home just two blocks from where the Baltimore Orioles' current ballpark sits, there were considerable challenges, as only young George and a sister, Mamie, survived to adulthood. Six other siblings succumbed to various causes.

Because Ruth's parents worked long hours to support the family, adult guidance was frequently lacking. As a result, George began causing problems at a very young age, disrupting the neighborhood and missing school with regularity. By the age of only seven, the future Bambino had become so difficult for his parents to control that they chose to enroll him at St. Mary's Industrial School for Boys in Baltimore, where the couple believed the regimented Catholic brothers would provide some much-needed structure for the irrepressible boy. It was there that young George began to turn his life around while learning to love a very special game. His structure would come from baseball.

Early on, Brother Matthias Boutilier, the school disciplinarian and himself a fair ballplayer, befriended Ruth in fatherly fashion and began to steer him in a positive direction. Boutilier's guidance included helping the youth refine his pitching, hitting, and catching skills, which would prove essential later in his life. It also involved inviting Baltimore Orioles owner Jack Dunn to a tryout of sorts. The owner was so impressed with the teen sensation's skill that after only one hour watching him perform, the club signed Ruth to a baseball contract that paid him six hundred dollars per season, a generous amount of money in those days. The year was 1914, and by 1915 Ruth would be on his way to fame, fortune, and a highly unorthodox career—in those early days mostly as a pitcher, not as the home-run-hitting outfielder that most people came to know.

The Baltimore Orioles players began referring to Ruth as "Jack's newest babe," a reference to Orioles owner Dunn, who adopted Ruth in order to sign him to a contract. Over time, the nickname was shortened and eventually stuck, and George Herman Ruth was forevermore known as simply the Babe—the most famous person ever to play the game.

After a brief stint with the Orioles during which he never played in a game, Ruth was sold to the Boston Red Sox in 1914, and for the next five years he played in Beantown, becoming a respected pitcher and feared hitter. However, he never hit more than twenty-nine home runs in a season until the Red Sox sold him to the Yankees in one of baseball's most colossal transactions after the 1919 season ended. Then, his stock began to soar.

After the Babe joined the Yankees in 1920, the club had an enviable decision to make. As a left-handed pitcher, Ruth had won ninety games in just over five seasons with the Red Sox, an average of eighteen per year, including twenty-three in 1916 and twenty-four in 1917, but the Yankees saw in him more value as a power hitter. Should Ruth hit every day, or should he pitch every fourth day, the team wondered? Finally, the decision was made by general manager Barrow, a former Red Sox manager who had come to the Yankees at the same time as Ruth; in 1920, his first season with the Yankees, Barrow, who had won a World Series managing in Boston, converted the Babe to a full-time hitter.

The gamble paid off handsomely for the Yankees and for Ruth. Playing every day in 1920, he led the American League in home runs with fifty-four and RBI with 135 while batting an astounding .376. People around the league took notice even though the Yankees failed to win a pennant.

After that, there was no stopping Ruth. He hit fifty-nine home runs the next year, led the league in batting with .378 in 1924, then hit sixty home runs in 1927, a mark that would stand for thirty-four years. During his remarkable career, Ruth was named MVP once (in 1923), led the league in home runs twelve times, and was the league leader in RBI five times. For seventeen consecutive seasons, Ruth hit ten or more home runs, four times hitting more than fifty, and twelve times slugging more than forty. In a 1999 ESPN poll, Ruth, an original member of the National Baseball Hall of Fame, was named the second-greatest athlete of the twentieth century behind former basketball superstar Michael Jordan.

Ruth mesmerized players and fans beyond the numbers he was able to accrue. In the 1932 World Series against the Cubs, he looked toward the outfield and famously pointed to a spot, believed to be near center field, where he predicted he would hit a home run. He didn't disappoint.

"[Cubs pitcher Charlie] Root throws it and I hit that (bleeping) ball on the nose—right over the (bleeping) fence for two (bleeping) runs," Ruth said, describing his called shot to famed sportswriter Grantland Rice. "How do you like those apples," Ruth yelled at Root as he trotted off to first following his famous called shot. Ruth told Rice, "By the time I reach home I'm almost fallin' down I'm laughin' so (bleeping) hard."[4]

In the 1926 World Series, Ruth reportedly promised to slug a home run for an ailing boy named John Dale Sylvester, who was suffering with a head infection that developed after a horse kicked him. Sylvester, who was eleven at the time, told his father, "I wish I could see Babe Ruth wallop a homer before I die." The Sylvester family wrote to the Yankees, who responded to the missive by sending the boy a baseball autographed by the Yankees and a second ball autographed by the team's competition in the World Series, the Cardinals. The slugger enclosed a note to the boy that undoubtedly lifted him onto the road to recovery: "I'll knock a homer for you on Wednesday," he wrote. Ruth, seldom one to fail his young fans, followed through on his promise and hit three home runs that day, to the delight of Sylvester, who went on to recover from the infection after a three-year struggle. He died in 1990 at the age of seventy-four—sixty-three years after Ruth called the shot.[5]

Ruth's estrangement from Gehrig probably began shortly before Ruth's career with the Yankees ended in 1934, although the exact circumstances remain uncertain. Some say it stemmed from Ruth's critical comments about Gehrig's consecutive games streak, which the Bambino felt was a sideshow that might actually be detrimental to the slugger. Others claim it began when Ruth's daughter visited Gehrig's mother while dressed inappropriately, offending the woman and prompting her to voice her opinion. Of the incident, Ruth wondered out loud why Mom Gehrig didn't mind her own business.[6] Still others believe the rift between the two resulted from disparaging comments Ruth made about the Yankees' manager McCarthy, which Gehrig resented. Whatever the reason for the chasm—perhaps it was a combination of the three—the players eventually broke off communication, although their performances on the field didn't suffer. In 1934, the aging Ruth's last year with the Yankees, he hit a commendable twenty-two home runs, drove in eighty-eight runners, and batted .288. Gehrig, meanwhile, hit forty-nine home runs, drove in 166 runners, and batted .363 to win his only batting crown in a near-MVP season.

Their relationship remained cool up until game time on Lou Gehrig Appreciation Day. Ruth arrived at the stadium later than many in the crowd had hoped he would, and there was some doubt as to whether he would even show up at all, given the strained nature of his relationship with the honoree. Suddenly, there he was, and the fans cheered approvingly as he slowly made his way from the grandstands along the infield to the turf near the batter's box, then finally over to the mass of microphones corralled near home plate. Mayor La Guardia spoke first, describing Gehrig as a model of both good citizenship and good sportsmanship. Then it was Postmaster Farley's turn, and he predicted with a sense of irony that Gehrig would "live long in baseball."[7] After the manager McCarthy expressed his sadness at losing Gehrig, it was Ruth's turn to speak, and he presented a tone of grace. Of the 1927 team, he said, "Lou was with us, and I say that was the greatest ball club the Yankees ever had."[8]

Finally, it was Gehrig's turn to speak, and he offered a humble yet brilliant oratory. When Gehrig was finished speaking, Ruth grabbed his teammate in a bear hug that warmed the hearts of those in attendance—including Gehrig. Then, the first baseman, at that moment officially a retired first baseman, smiled, walked away, and vanished into the Yankees dugout, leaving the organization to flourish on its own—watered through the years by his undying legacy.

"To be a Yankee today, there's a responsibility to uphold the past," former Yankee Mike Buddie said. "If you play for the Yankees, it just means more because people like Lou Gehrig changed the game through their humanity. There's an expectation that when you have a platform and a stage like you're afforded as a New York Yankee, you should use it to make the world a better place. I think that's what Lou's speech probably epitomized. For it to have caught on and affected the entire world as it has says a lot about the impact that it had."[9]

The small circle of people who understood the seriousness of Gehrig's illness, including Eleanor and Barrow, knew the slugger's days could be numbered. What they didn't know was that Ruth would soon face his own painful battle for survival.

Figure E.2. Babe Ruth, in this instance a fan, attends a ball game, 1922. Library of Congress, National Photo Company Collection.

When a loved one dies, healing often begins in earnest after the funeral. That's not always so. More than eighty years after Gehrig's death, the healing continues and to some extent probably always will, despite efforts to mitigate his demise. Those efforts have largely failed, for the world will always lament Gehrig's premature passing and the years of quality baseball his disease may have stolen—no matter how many postage stamps display his portrait, or pets are assigned the name "Lou," or Little League ball fields are christened "Lou Gehrig Park."

Consider the following timeline of events that have occurred since Gehrig's untimely death in 1941. Combined, they paint a picture of a man increasingly beloved as the years have ticked by—perhaps even more so today than ever:

> June 3, 1941. Gehrig's former boss, Mayor La Guardia, orders flags across New York City lowered to half-staff.
>
> June 4, 1941. Gehrig's funeral is held at Christ Episcopal Church in the Bronx, and he is buried at Kensico Cemetery, with an incorrect birth date etched onto his headstone. The Yankees erect a monument to Gehrig behind the center-field fence at Yankee Stadium.
>
> 1941–1945. Eleanor and others donate ambulances to New York City. The vehicles have the lettering "Lou Gehrig Memorial" affixed to their sides. Baseball fields from coast to coast are renamed for Gehrig. His name is attached to a liberty ship.
>
> 1950. Yankees broadcaster Mel Allen donates money for the establishment of a scholarship fund honoring Gehrig at Columbia University.
>
> August 21, 1953. A memorial plaque is placed outside Gehrig's birthplace, which by then has been converted into a laundromat.
>
> 1969. Gehrig is voted greatest first baseman ever by the Baseball Writers' Association of America.
>
> 1989. The US Postal Service memorializes Gehrig with a twenty-five-cent postage stamp.
>
> May 27, 1995. Pitcher Curt Schilling, a future six-time All-Star, names his son Gehrig Schilling.

September 20, 1998. When Cal Ripken Jr. breaks Gehrig's consecutive games streak, the crowd chants "Lou, Lou."

May 2000. The ALS Association begins a comprehensive research project designed to vigorously investigate the disease.

May 31, 2002. More than a dozen ballparks across the country hold Project ALS Day, with celebrities reading a presumed version of Gehrig's speech at home plate.[10]

If time heals all wounds, then what about the cavernous gash created by Lou Gehrig's death? Where Gehrig is concerned, there are few left who can truly answer that question. Bobby Doerr, believed to be the last man living who had played against Gehrig, died in 2017 at the age of ninety-nine. The Red Sox star made his first of nine All-Star Game appearances in 1941, the year of Gehrig's death.

Tommy Henrich, the last surviving teammate to have played alongside Gehrig, died in 2009 at the age of ninety-six. Henrich, himself a five-time All-Star, was the last player alive who heard Gehrig utter the memorable words *"Today I consider myself the luckiest man on the face of the earth."*

Henrich may have been the last player standing, but he wasn't the last person alive who heard those famous words. Brooklyn native Vinnie Anella, now ninety, was only seven years old when his father took him to Yankee Stadium to celebrate Independence Day in 1939. While his memories of that event have faded, Anella does recall seeing Ruth hug Gehrig to melt the duo's long-standing discomfiture. "I was standing up when [Ruth] came out [onto the field]; everyone was screaming and yelling," said Anella, one of a vanishing fraternity of eyewitnesses.[11]

Anella attended the game with his father, and the two viewed the ceremony from the reserved section along the first baseline just beyond the Yankees dugout. Six years later, the pair would travel to nearby Ebbets Field to watch Jackie Robinson's historic first game in the big leagues. One year after that, in 1948, Anella's father would invite his son to see Babe Ruth lying in an open casket at Yankee Stadium following the baseball legend's death from cancer. The boy, by then a teenager, didn't understand the importance of that opportunity, and he declined to go along. Still, no one can remove July 4, 1939, from Anella's distant memory bank, nor his admiration for Gehrig. "He was a great baseball player," said Anella, who now lives in Viera, Florida. "[The speech] was a classic."[12]

Great ballplayer. Classic speech. In a nutshell, that sums up Lou Gehrig and his "Luckiest Man" farewell. In the context of unforgettable sports oratories, Gehrig's was unparalleled, one that spotlighted for all time his calm spirit while under duress, his flawless character, and his overarching importance to the New York Yankees organization and the game of baseball. In that regard, little has changed—neither Gehrig's legendary persona nor his impact both on the Yankees and on a child's game played with bat and ball.

Perhaps Postmaster James Farley, who spoke prior to Gehrig that day, summed up the slugger's speech better than anyone in a letter he wrote to the Iron Horse the following day, on July 5, 1939: "Your speech was magnificent. . . . You did not overlook a thing. Your reference to your team, to your wife, to your parents, and everyone else to whom you referred showed, despite the strain you were under, that you had your eye on the ball."[13]

For better or for worse, the spotlight on Gehrig's speech—with or without inclusion of the indefatigable Ruth—hasn't dimmed since Farley penned those astute observations. After all the years, after all the tears, Gehrig's legacy remains intact, etched forever as his Bronx epitaph.

AFTERWORD

> We are like butterflies who flutter for a day and think it's forever.
>
> —Carl Sagan

After July 4, 1939, time passed tortuously for Lou Gehrig. He battled ALS through an endless maze of doctor appointments, hospital examinations, and appointments to positions he knew he'd be unable to fulfill. Finally, at 10:10 p.m. on June 2, 1941, Gehrig's body gave out, and he passed away at his home, 5204 Delafield Avenue, the Bronx. In a story announcing his death, one sportswriter described him as perhaps the greatest player who ever lived but a man whose career was cut short by a type of chronic paralysis that left him homebound during his final month of life, a time when his weight continued to drop and, finally, he was confined to bed. Gehrig, the newspaper reported, lost consciousness shortly before he passed away with his wife, parents, and a doctor at his bedside.[1]

In the months before he died, the rapidly failing Gehrig had spent countless hours seated at home in an easy chair next to his front window, gazing out at the street and likely wondering how his future would play out. Even then, not knowing the full extent of his illness, he had an inkling. Up until the very end, one of his most cherished possessions was the trophy he received from his teammates on Lou Gehrig Appreciation Day.

Services for Gehrig were held at Christ Episcopal Church in the Bronx, and the slugger was interred at Kensico Cemetery in Valhalla, New York, where fans, many of whom were not even born when the Iron Horse played for the Yankees, still leave bats, balls, gloves, and caps at his grave. Honorary pallbearers included Yankees catcher and Gehrig devotee Bill Dickey, the manager McCarthy, and the legendary dancer

Bill "Bojangles" Robinson, who had tapped alongside Shirley Temple in *Rebecca of Sunnybrook Farm* just three years earlier.

"He was one of the greatest players ever," said former Yankee Greg Cadaret. "I had heard his history and I respected it from day one."[2]

Over time, the malady that riddled him was dubbed Lou Gehrig's disease in the slugger's memory. Today, ALS remains a medical conundrum—much like Gehrig's simple, heartfelt speech delivered to the baseball masses on Independence Day in 1939. For Gehrig, independence came on June 2, 1941—the day he died peacefully at home.

After her husband's funeral, Eleanor Gehrig extended considerable effort both ensuring that his legacy remained intact and filling the huge void that his death had created in her own life. For years she served as his official spokeswoman and a golden link between Gehrig and his many fans. Publicly, she was seldom introduced as Eleanor Gehrig; rather, "Mrs. Lou Gehrig" became her primary identity. Although she cherished that connection, possibly as a result of it she never remarried.

As time passed Eleanor was asked to address various tributes to Gehrig, and requests came in for her to help raise funds for a number of causes, present speeches, and cut ribbons. With all the busyness that had enveloped her life, she privately worried that the peace she longed for would always elude her. For much of the rest of her life, it did.

Through the years, her relationship with Gehrig's parents remained strained. Heinrich and Christina eventually sued Eleanor for interest payments that they believed were being withheld from a life insurance policy their son had left behind. A settlement was reached two years later; however, the relationship never improved. The three even squabbled about the disposition of his ashes.

When Gehrig's cinematic biography *The Pride of the Yankees* was conceptualized, Eleanor was on the front line, selling to film producer Samuel Goldwyn the rights to her late husband's story in exchange for a sum reportedly totaling thirty thousand dollars.[3] While Gary Cooper was a lock to play the part of Gehrig, Eleanor believed Teresa Wright was too young to portray Mrs. Lou Gehrig. She suggested that other actresses might be more appropriate; however, Wright was young and sweet and in the end was given the coveted role[4]—for which she, like Cooper, earned an Academy Award. Goldwyn received an Oscar for Best Picture.

As World War II dragged on, Eleanor leveraged Gehrig's squeaky-clean image to sell war bonds[5] and eventually sold some of his coveted baseball memorabilia for a reported six million dollars. She also received a presidential citation for selflessly joining the American Red Cross[6] and for helping to drive disabled Americans to their destinations.

Perhaps most meaningful, at least from a personal standpoint, was Eleanor's support for research aimed at finding a cure for ALS. A portion of her estate was designated to support research into the causes and effects of, and certainly a cure for, paralytic diseases, and the Eleanor and Lou Gehrig MDA/ALS Multidisciplinary Care Center at the New York-Presbyterian Hospital/Columbia University is a lasting tribute. Columbia University's Irving Medical Center today hosts the Eleanor and Lou Gehrig ALS Center.

Eventually, the solitude Eleanor sought in widowhood turned into loneliness, and her mother moved in with her as a companion in downtown New York City. In 1982, many years after her mother's death, Eleanor nearly burned down her apartment when she dropped a lighted cigarette onto her mattress.[7] Finally, the woman known as Lou Gehrig's wife died two years later, on her eightieth birthday. Only two mourners attended the funeral: her attorney, George Pollack, and his wife, Dorothy.

Following their son's death in 1941, Christina and Heinrich Gehrig enjoyed heightened popularity, especially when *The Pride of the Yankees* was released in 1942. Four years later, Mom Gehrig mourned her husband's death, then moved briefly to Milford, Connecticut, in 1948. Once there, she mobilized to help organize the Milford Little League, joining the board of directors, attending all of its meetings, and often sitting alone to watch the various Milford teams play. As ever, Christina loved baseball in any form, and with Lou gone her attention shifted to the sport's lowest tier: Little League. As a result of her commitment to the community, Milford Little League teams now compete at Lou Gehrig Field, renamed such in 1952—two years before Mom Gehrig's own death on December 2, 1954. She is buried next to her husband, who lived quietly with his wife for five years after Gehrig died, and their son at Kensico Cemetery. The deaths of Mom and Pop Gehrig marked an end to perhaps the most famous parental duo in sports history.

∽

Involvement in a funeral service speaks volumes about a person's relationship with the deceased. In April 1938, Jacob Ruppert's health had begun to deteriorate, largely due to phlebitis and later to a serious liver ailment. The gravity of his health issues became abundantly clear when he failed to attend the 1938 World Series, which his Yankees swept in four games over the Cubs. Finally, on January 4, 1939, Ruppert suffered a serious heart attack and died ten days later. With Babe Ruth present in the room when he passed, the colonel's last word was "Babe."[8]

Ruppert's funeral was held at St. Patrick's Cathedral in New York City, and honorary pallbearers encompassed a who's who of baseball and political luminaries. Included were Commissioner Kenesaw Mountain Landis, Yankees manager Joe McCarthy, Yankees general manager Ed Barrow, Babe Ruth, Yankees farm system director George Weiss, United States senator Robert Wagner of New York, former New York governor Al Smith, American League president Will Harridge, National League president Ford Frick, former National League president and Pennsylvania governor John Tenor, former congressman and Boston mayor John F. "Honey Fitz" Fitzgerald (grandfather of future president John F. Kennedy), and Gehrig. In death, as in life, Gehrig and Ruppert maintained a special bond. It's no surprise, then, that Larrupin' Lou remembered Ruppert in his "Luckiest Man" speech, asking the crowd, "*Who wouldn't consider it an honor to have known Jacob Ruppert?*" Clearly, Gehrig did.

Ed Barrow retired from baseball five years after Gehrig's death and the same year that Pop Gehrig passed away, in 1946, but not before presiding over two world championships in the post-Gehrig era, in 1941 and 1943. During his final World Series, Barrow was stricken with a heart attack; however, he eventually recovered and lived another highly productive decade. While his retirement from the sport was relatively brief, it was not inconsequential: he proudly worked as a member of the National Baseball Hall of Fame committee that was charged with considering for enshrinement ballplayers whom the baseball writers failed to induct in traditional balloting. Finally, after suffering with ill health for a number of years, Barrow died in December 1953 at the age of eighty-five, just weeks after being named to the Hall of Fame himself. He was buried at the same cemetery where Gehrig and his parents are interred, in Valhalla, New York.

∽

After Gehrig's death in 1941, Joe McCarthy managed in the major leagues for another eight years—five with the Yankees and three with the Red Sox—before retiring after the 1950 season (he did not manage in 1947). He won four more pennants, in 1942, 1943, 1947, and 1949, and three world championships, in 1943, 1947, and 1949. During his final season with Boston, McCarthy led the Red Sox to a 94–60 finish and third place in the American League. Over twenty-four seasons as a major-league manager with the Cubs, Yankees, and Red Sox, McCarthy won 2,125 games and lost 1,333 for a winning percentage of .615—and seven world championships. McCarthy's teams never performed under .500 and never finished worse than fourth place, and his career regular-season and postseason winning percentages are the best of any manager in history.

McCarthy resigned from the Red Sox in 1950 due to poor health, returning instead to his upstate New York farm, where he kept busy gardening and overseeing repairs. His wife died at the farm in 1971, and McCarthy succumbed to pneumonia at a nearby hospital eight years later at the age of ninety; his final resting place is Mount Olivet Cemetery in Tonawanda, not far from where his farm was located. McCarthy lived long enough to see himself voted into the National Baseball Hall of Fame in 1957 by the organization's Veterans Committee.

Sometime around 1945, Babe Ruth began experiencing neck pain and headaches, and doctors diagnosed him with throat cancer. He continued on as best he could despite the pain he would suffer over the last two years of his life: he wrote a book, became one of the first patients to undergo chemotherapy combined with radiation therapy, and made one final appearance in uniform at Yankee Stadium on June 13, 1948, his number-three jersey and pants hanging loosely on his failing body. Speaking with a hoarse, difficult-to-understand voice as he leaned against one of Bob Feller's bats, Ruth told the crowd, "If you're successful and you try hard enough, you're bound to come out on top."

Less than two months later, on August 16, 1948, Ruth died; his funeral—like Ruppert's—was held at St. Patrick's Cathedral in New York City. In 1985, St. Patrick's would also be the site of a requiem mass for Roger Maris, the man who in 1961 broke the Babe's single-season home-run mark. As was fitting for a man of Ruth's larger-than-life stature, there were fifty-seven honorary pallbearers at his service, including former world heavyweight boxing champion Jack Dempsey, the dancer Bill "Bojangles" Robinson, New York mayor William O'Dwyer, longtime Philadelphia Athletics manager Connie Mack, former newspaper columnist and future television variety show host Ed Sullivan, former teammate Frank Crosetti, Yankee great DiMaggio, and actor William Bendix, who played Ruth in *The Babe Ruth Story*.

On April 27, 1947, in a short speech during Babe Ruth Day at Yankee Stadium, Ruth, speaking in a gravelly voice, finally had an opportunity to publicly say thanks for "so many lovely things said about me" and added, "I'm glad that I've had the opportunity to thank everybody." Gehrig, of course, had gone a step further, declaring himself "*the luckiest man on the face of the earth.*" Neither man, certainly, was lucky at the end, Gehrig dying from ALS and Ruth from nasopharyngeal cancer. With Ruth's passing less than four months after Babe Ruth Day and seven years after Gehrig, the Ruth-Gehrig era was officially over.

Bill Dickey, Gehrig's closest friend, remained a steadfast companion during the two years that he battled ALS. After sitting out the 1944 and 1945 seasons due to military service, Dickey rejoined the Yankees in 1946 and batted .261 with 134 at bats before retiring as a player. When McCarthy abruptly retired thirty-five games into the 1946 season, Dickey took the helm and finished with an 87–67 record—well out of the money. He managed in the minor leagues the following season, then returned to the big club to help refine the rookie Yogi Berra's catching skills; thanks in part to Dickey's tutelage, Berra, like his mentor, was eventually elected to the Hall of Fame. Meanwhile, Dickey never managed again. He was enshrined in the National Baseball Hall of Fame in 1954 and died in Arkansas at the age of eighty-six in 1993; one of his biggest regrets was the premature death of Gehrig. The two never had a chance to grow old together as pals.

When loneliness overcame her daughter following Gehrig's death, Nellie Twitchell moved in with Eleanor to help even out the rough spots. She died in 1968, leaving Eleanor once again all alone. Eleanor remained that way until her own death sixteen years later.

APPENDIX

LOU GEHRIG'S "LUCKIEST MAN" SPEECH

Fans, for the past two weeks you've been reading about a bad break. Today I consider myself the luckiest man on the face of the earth.[1] I've been walking into ballparks for seventeen years and have never received anything but kindness and encouragement from you fans.[2] Mine has been a full life.[3] Newspapers have said nice things about me, which I found hard to believe myself.[4] When you look around, wouldn't you consider it a privilege to associate yourself with such fine-looking men as are standing in uniform in this ballpark today?[5] Sure, I'm lucky.[6] Who wouldn't consider it an honor to have known Jacob Ruppert?[7] Also, the builder of baseball's greatest empire, Ed Barrow?[8] To have spent six years with such a grand little fellow as Miller Huggins?[9] To have spent the next nine years with that master psychologist, the greatest manager in baseball today, Joe McCarthy?[10] And when you have the privilege of rooming, eating, playing cards, and knowing one of the greatest fellows that ever lived, my roommate, Bill Dickey.[11] When the fellows from across the river, the New York Giants, a team you would give your right arm to beat, and vice versa, sends a gift, that's something.[12] It's something to be remembered by a rival organization.[13] When the groundskeepers and office staff and writers and old timers and players and those boys in white coats all remember you with trophies, that's something.[14] When you have a mother-in-law who takes sides with you in squabbles against her own daughter—that's really something.[15] When you have a father and a mother who work all their lives so that you can have an education and build your body, it's a blessing.[16] When you have a wonderful wife who has been a tower of strength show more courage than I ever dreamed existed—that's the finest thing I know.[17] So I close in saying that I might've been given a bad break, but I've got an awful lot to live for. Thank you.[18]

PORTIONS OF LOU GEHRIG'S SPEECH CAPTURED ON VIDEO[19]

For the past two weeks you've been reading about a bad break. Today I consider myself the luckiest man on the face of the earth.

. . .

When you look around, wouldn't you consider it a privilege to associate yourself with such fine-looking men as are standing in uniform in this ballpark today?

. . .

. . . that I might've been given a bad break, but I've got an awful lot to live for.

LETTER FROM THE MAYO CLINIC ANNOUNCING LOU GEHRIG'S ALS DIAGNOSIS[20]

June 19, 1939

To Whom it May Concern,

This is to certify that Mr. Lou Gehrig has been under examination at the Mayo Clinic from June 13 to June 19, 1939, inclusive.

After a careful and complete examination, it was found that he is suffering from amyotrophic lateral sclerosis. This type of illness involves the motor pathways and cells of the central nervous system and in lay terms is known as a form of chronic poliomyelitis [infantile paralysis].

The nature of this trouble makes it such that Mr. Gehrig will be unable to continue his active participation as a baseball player inasmuch as it is advisable that he conserve his muscular energy. He could, however, continue in some executive capacity.

Signed,

Harold C. Habein, M.D.

Table A.1. Lou Gehrig's Final Game, April 30, 1939

Batting	AB	R	H	RBI	BB	SO	AVG
Crosetti, ss	5	0	0	0	0	2	.147
Rolfe, 3b	4	1	1	0	1	0	.242
Powell, cf	3	0	0	0	0	0	.273
Henrich, cf	1	0	0	0	0	1	.200
Dickey, c	2	0	1	0	2	0	.417
Gehrig, 1b	4	0	0	0	0	0	.143
Gallagher, rf	3	1	1	0	0	1	.222
Keller, rf	0	0	0	0	1	0	.200
Selkirk, lf	3	0	0	1	1	0	.214
Gordon, 2b	3	0	0	0	1	1	.136
Hildebrand, p	2	0	1	1	0	0	.250
Murphy, p	0	0	0	0	0	0	—
Ruffing, ph	1	0	0	0	0	0	.167
Team Totals	31	2	4	2	6	5	.129

Source: "Washington Senators at New York Yankees Box Score, April 30, 1939," Baseball Reference, accessed September 20, 2019, https://www.baseball-reference.com/boxes/NYA/NYA193904300.shtml.

AB, at bats; R, runs scored/allowed; H, hits/hits allowed; RBI, runs batted in; BB, bases on balls/walks; SO, strikeouts; AVG, hits/at bats (batting average); ss, shortstop; 3b, third baseman; cf, center fielder; c, catcher; 1b, first baseman; rf, right fielder; lf, left fielder; 2b, second baseman; p, pitcher; ph, pinch hitter.

Table A.2. Lou Gehrig's Minor-League Statistics

Season	Team	Level	AB	H	2B	3B	HR	RBI	AVG
1921	Hartford	A	46	12	1	2	0	N/A	.261
1923	Hartford	A	227	69	13	8	24	N/A	.304
1924	Hartford	A	504	186	40	13	37	N/A	.369
Totals			777	267	54	23	61	—	.343

Source: "Lou Gehrig: Minor Lg Stats," Baseball Reference, accessed April 16, 2019, https://www.baseball-reference.com/register/player.fcgi?id=gehrig001hen.

AB, at bats; H, hits/hits allowed; 2B, doubles hit/allowed; 3B, triples hit/allowed; HR, home runs; RBI, runs batted in; AVG, hits/at bats (batting average).

Table A.3. Lou Gehrig's Major-League Statistics

Season	Team	League	AB	H	2B	3B	HR	RBI	AVG
1923	NYY	AL	26	11	4	1	1	8	.423
1924	NYY	AL	12	6	1	0	0	5	.500
1925	NYY	AL	437	129	23	10	20	68	.295
1926	NYY	AL	572	179	47	20	16	109	.313
1927	NYY	AL	584	218	52	18	47	173	.373
1928	NYY	AL	562	210	47	13	27	147	.374
1929	NYY	AL	553	166	32	10	35	125	.300
1930	NYY	AL	581	220	42	17	41	173	.379
1931	NYY	AL	619	211	31	15	46	185	.341
1932	NYY	AL	596	208	42	9	34	151	.349
1933	NYY	AL	593	198	41	12	32	140	.334
1934	NYY	AL	579	210	40	6	49	166	.363
1935	NYY	AL	535	176	26	10	30	120	.329
1936	NYY	AL	579	205	37	7	49	152	.354
1937	NYY	AL	569	200	37	9	37	158	.351
1938	NYY	AL	576	170	32	6	29	114	.295
1939	NYY	AL	28	4	0	0	0	1	.143
Totals			8,001	2,721	534	163	493	1,995	.340

Source: "Lou Gehrig: Overview," Baseball Reference, accessed February 8, 2017, http://www.baseball-reference.com/players/g/gehrilo01.shtml.

NYY, New York Yankees; AL, American League; AB, at bats; H, hits/hits allowed; 2B, doubles hit/allowed; 3B, triples hit/allowed; HR, home runs; RBI, runs batted in; AVG, hits/at bats (batting average).

Table A.4. Johnny Welaj's Major-League Statistics

Season	Team	League	AB	H	2B	3B	HR	RBI	AVG
1939	WS	AL	201	55	11	2	1	33	.274
1940	WS	AL	215	55	9	0	3	21	.256
1941	WS	AL	96	20	4	0	0	5	.208
1943	PHA	AL	281	68	16	1	0	15	.242
Totals			**793**	**198**	**40**	**3**	**4**	**74**	**.250**

Source: "Johnny Welaj: Overview," Baseball Reference, accessed May 10, 2019, https://www.baseball-reference.com/players/w/welajjo01.shtml.

WS, Washington Senators; PHA, Philadelphia Athletics; AL, American League; AB, at bats; H, hits/hits allowed; 2B, doubles hit/allowed; 3B, triples hit/allowed; HR, home runs; RBI, runs batted in; AVG, hits/at bats (batting average).

NOTES

PREFACE

1. "Gehrig Delivers His Famous Speech at Yankee Stadium," filmed July 4, 1939, video, 1:09, https://www.youtube.com/watch?v=nNLKPaThYkE.

2. Shirley Povich, "This Morning with Shirley Povich: 'Iron Horse' Breaks as Athletic Greats Meet in His Honor," *Washington Post*, July 4, 1939, reprinted August 27, 1995, https://www.washingtonpost.com/wp-srv/sports/longterm/general/povich/launch/gehrig39.htm.

3. Edward T. Murphy, "History of Baseball: Iron Man Is Moved to Tears," *New York Sun*, July 5, 1939, 29.

4. Rosaleen Doherty, "Lou Gehrig Retires, Gives 'Luckiest Man on the Face of the Earth' Speech at Yankee Stadium in 1939," *New York Daily News*, July 3, 2015, https://www.nydailynews.com/services/new-york-then-now/bronx/sports-rewind-lou-gehrig-retires-luckiest-man-article-1.2041915.

5. Doherty, "Lou Gehrig Retires."

6. Sid Feder, "Lou Gehrig Sobs as 62,000 Pay Tribute," *San Diego Union*, July 4, 1939 (sourced from the Associated Press); Doherty, "Lou Gehrig Retires."

7. Rud Rennie, "Ailing First Baseman, Sobbing after Honors by La Guardia and Farley, Thrills Stadium Throng as He Calls Himself Luckiest Man on Earth," *New York Herald Tribune*, July 5, 1939.

8. Doherty, "Lou Gehrig Retires"; Povich, "'Iron Horse' Breaks."

9. Stanley Frank, "Tribute Paid to Iron Horse Has No Equal in Baseball," *New York Post*, July 5, 1939.

10. Doherty, "Lou Gehrig Retires."

11. Feder, "Lou Gehrig Sobs"; Doherty, "Lou Gehrig Retires."

12. Doherty, "Lou Gehrig Retires."

13. Frank, "Tribute"; Doherty, "Lou Gehrig Retires."

14. Eliot Asinof, *Eight Men Out: The Black Sox and the 1919 World Series* (New York: Henry Holt, 1963), 189.

INTRODUCTION

1. "Luckiest Man," National Baseball Hall of Fame and Museum, accessed March 23, 2019, https://baseballhall.org/discover-more/stories/baseball-history/lou-gehrig-luckiest-man.

2. Steve Wulf, "An Awful Lot to Live For," *ESPN*, July 3, 2014, http://www.espn.com/mlb/story/_/id/11159148/mlb-remembering-lou-gehrig-farewell-speech.

3. Rosaleen Doherty, "Lou Gehrig Retires, Gives 'Luckiest Man on the Face of the Earth' Speech at Yankee Stadium in 1939," *New York Daily News*, July 3, 2015, https://www.nydailynews.com/services/new-york-then-now/bronx/sports-rewind-lou-gehrig-retires-luckiest-man-article-1.2041915.

4. Irv Noren, interviewed by the author, October 24, 2019.

5. Frank Graham, *Lou Gehrig: A Quiet Hero* (Eau Claire, WI: E. M. Hale, 1942), 6–7.

6. Graham, *Lou Gehrig*, 55.

7. "Quotes by Lou Gehrig," LouGehrig.com, accessed February 8, 2017, http://lougehrig.com/about/quotes.html.

8. "Quotes."

9. "By and about Lou Gehrig," ESPN Classic, November 19, 2003, accessed August 18, 2020, http://www.espn.com/classic/s/gehrigmartinquotes000809.html; "Quotes by Lou Gehrig," LouGehrig.com, accessed March 10, 2017, http://lougehrig.com/about/quotes.html.

10. Irv Noren, interviewed by the author, October 24, 2019.

11. Wulf, "Awful Lot."

12. Al Schacht, *Clowning through Baseball* (New York: A. S. Barnes, 1941).

13. Steven Goldman, "75 Years Later, Babe Ruth's Hug Means Almost As Much As Lou Gehrig's Speech," *SB Nation*, July 8, 2014, https://www.sbnation.com/mlb/2014/7/8/5878847/lou-gehrig-babe-ruth-75-anniverary-luckiest-man-speech-forgiveness-history.

CHAPTER 1

1. "Steve Sax," They Were There: The TGG Interviews, *This Great Game: The Online Book of Baseball*, accessed April 2, 2019, http://www.thisgreatgame.com/steve-sax.html.

2. Bobby Shantz, interviewed by the author, November 25, 2019.

3. Sara Kaden, "High School Hero Gehrig," *MoreGehrig: Extensive Gehrig Info Source*, accessed March 21, 2019, http://moregehrig.tripod.com/id24.html.

4. Roger Repoz, interviewed by the author, November 19, 2019.

5. "Classic Sports Presents Lou Gehrig July 4, 1939," television clip uploaded to YouTube May 8, 2018 by Max Carey, https://www.youtube.com/watch?v=Oj2Fmr-W-t8.

6. Frank Graham, *Lou Gehrig: A Quiet Hero* (Eau Claire, WI: E. M. Hale, 1942), 68.

7. Harvey Frommer, *Five O'Clock Lightning: Babe Ruth, Lou Gehrig, and the Greatest Team in Baseball, the 1927 New York Yankees* (Hoboken, NJ: John Wiley & Sons, 2008), 94.

8. James Lincoln Ray, "Lou Gehrig," Society for American Baseball Research, accessed April 2, 2019, https://sabr.org/bioproj/person/lou-gehrig/.

9. Adam Brunner and Josh Leventhal, eds., *The Yankees Baseball Reader: A Collection of Writings on the Game's Greatest Dynasty* (Minneapolis, MN: MVP Books, 2011), 79.

10. Robert Greenberger, *Lou Gehrig* (New York: Rosen Central, 2003).

11. Sara Kaden, "More about His ALS Battle," *MoreGehrig: Extensive Gehrig Info Source*, 2002, accessed March 29, 2019, http://moregehrig.tripod.com/id3.html.

12. Repoz, interviewed by the author, November 19, 2019.

13. Dom Amore, "Speech Class: 75 Years Ago, a Dignified Lou Gehrig Bows Out," *Morning Call*, July 7, 2014, accessed May 1, 2019, https://www.mcall.com/sports/mc-xpm-2014-07-07-mc-lou-gehrig-speech-anniversary-yankees-0707-20140707-story.html.

14. Graham, *Lou Gehrig*, 232–33.

15. Herbert L. Fred, "Lou Gehrig and Ed Todd: Greatness Interrupted," *Texas Heart Institute Journal* 44, no. 6 (December 2017): 383, https://www.ncbi.nlm.nih.gov/pmc/articles/PMC5737147/.

16. Sara Kaden Brunsvold, *The Life of Lou Gehrig: Told by a Fan* (Chicago: ACTA Sports, 2006).

17. Shantz, interviewed by the author, November 24, 2019.

CHAPTER 2

1. James M. Kahn, quoted in Gene Elston, *A Stitch in Time: A Baseball Chronology, 1845–2002* (Houston, TX: Halcyon Press, 2006), 189.

2. Andy McGaffigan, interviewed by the author, October 10, 2019.

3. James Lincoln Ray, "Lou Gehrig," Society for American Baseball Research, accessed July 22, 2019, https://sabr.org/bioproj/person/lou-gehrig/.

CHAPTER 3

1. Andy McGaffigan, interviewed by the author, October 10, 2019.

2. Jane Leavy, *The Last Boy: Mickey Mantle and the End of America's Childhood* (New York: Harper Perennial, 2011).

3. "Lou Gehrig Quotes," Baseball Almanac, accessed July 31, 2019, https://www.baseball-almanac.com/quotes/quogehr.shtml.

4. Andy McGaffigan, interviewed by the author, October 10, 2019.
5. "Lou Gehrig Quotes."
6. "Lou Gehrig Quotes."
7. "Lou Gehrig Quotes."
8. McGaffigan, interviewed by the author, October 10, 2019.
9. Fred Kipp, interviewed by the author, November 19, 2019.
10. "Letter from Harold C. Habein, M.D. to Whom It May Concern, 1939 June 19," National Baseball Hall of Fame and Museum digital collection, accessed September 20, 2020 (see appendix).
11. Shirley Povich, "This Morning with Shirley Povich: 'Iron Horse' Breaks as Athletic Greats Meet in His Honor," *Washington Post*, July 4, 1939; quoted in Mike Vaccaro, "Portrait in Courage—History's Lucky an Ailing Gehrig Stepped Up to Plate One Last Time," *New York Post*, July 4, 2004, https://nypost.com/2004/07/04/portrait-in-courage-historys-lucky-an-ailing-gehrig-stepped-up-to-plate-one-last-time/.
12. Rick Dempsey, interviewed by the author, October 30, 2019.

CHAPTER 4

1. "Looking Back at Lou Gehrig Appreciation Day," JUGS Sports blog, August 28, 2018, https://jugssports.com/looking-back-at-lou-gehrig-appreciation-day/.
2. Christine Daniels, "1927 Yankees," *Los Angeles Times*, January 27, 2008, https://www.latimes.com/archives/la-xpm-2008-jan-27-sp-daniels27-story.html.
3. "Tony Lazzeri," National Baseball Hall of Fame, accessed June 7, 2019, https://baseballhall.org/hall-of-famers/lazzeri-tony.

CHAPTER 5

1. Bill Virdon, interviewed by the author, November 15, 2019.
2. Frank Graham, *Lou Gehrig: A Quiet Hero* (Eau Claire, WI: E. M. Hale, 1942), 55.
3. Steve Steinberg and Lyle Spatz, *The Colonel and Hug: The Partnership That Transformed the New York Yankees* (Lincoln: University of Nebraska Press, 2015), 16.
4. James Lincoln Ray, "Lou Gehrig," Society for American Baseball Research, accessed April 3, 2019, https://sabr.org/bioproj/person/lou-gehrig/.
5. Virdon, interviewed by the author, November 15, 2019.
6. Frank Graham, *The New York Yankees: An Informal History* (New York: Editions for the Armed Services, 1943), 151.
7. Steinberg and Spatz, *Colonel and Hug*, 304.

8. James Lincoln Ray, "Lou Gehrig," Society for American Baseball Research, accessed April 3, 2019, https://sabr.org/bioproj/person/lou-gehrig/.
9. Ray Robinson, *Iron Horse: Lou Gehrig in His Time* (New York: W. W. Norton, 1990), 232.
10. Robinson, *Iron Horse*, 234.
11. Robinson, 235.

CHAPTER 6

1. Bill Virdon, interviewed by the author, November 15, 2019.
2. Ray Robinson, *Iron Horse: Lou Gehrig in His Time* (New York: W. W. Norton, 1990), 134.
3. "Ed Barrow," National Baseball Hall of Fame and Museum, accessed April 24, 2019, https://baseballhall.org/hall-of-famers/barrow-ed/.
4. "Yanks Never to Use Gehrig's 'No. 4' Again," January 7, 1940, in Dave Anderson and Bill Pennington, eds., *The New York Times Story of the Yankees, 1903–Present: 390 Articles, Profiles & Essays* (New York: Black Dog & Leventhal Publishers, 2012), 103.
5. David Schoenfield, "The Greatest General Managers of All Time," February 13, 2015, ESPN, https://www.espn.com/blog/sweetspot/post/_/id/55105/the-greatest-general-managers-of-all-time.

CHAPTER 7

1. "Hug Class of Bunch as Pilot, Says Gehrig," *New York American*, September 28, 1927, quoted in Steve Steinberg, "Miller Huggins," Society for American Baseball Research, accessed April 16, 2019, https://sabr.org/bioproj/person/miller-huggins/.
2. Gil Patterson, interviewed by the author, November 4, 2019.
3. James R. Harrison, "Baseball," *New York Times*, March 8, 1926, quoted in Steinberg, "Miller Huggins."
4. "Hug Guards Yanks against Let-Down," *Sporting News*, August 4, 1927, quoted in Steinberg.
5. Frank Graham, *Lou Gehrig: A Quiet Hero* (Eau Claire, WI: E. M. Hale, 1942), 94.
6. Tony Castro, *Gehrig & the Babe: The Friendship and the Feud* (Chicago, IL: Triumph Books, 2018), 14.
7. Ray Robinson, *Iron Horse: Lou Gehrig in His Time* (New York: W. W. Norton, 1990), 101.
8. Robinson, *Iron Horse*, 105.
9. Graham, *Lou Gehrig*, 130.

10. Graham, 131.

11. Paul Warburton, *Signature Seasons: Fifteen Baseball Legends at Their Most Memorable, 1908–1949* (Jefferson, NC: McFarland, 2010), 132.

CHAPTER 8

1. Brad Engel and Wayne Stewart, *Tales from First Base: The Best, Funniest, and Slickest First Basemen Ever* (Washington, DC: Potomac Books, 2013), 60.

2. Shirley Povich, "This Morning with Shirley Povich: 'Iron Horse' Breaks as Athletic Greats Meet in His Honor," *Washington Post*, July 4, 1939, reprinted August 27, 1995, https://www.washingtonpost.com/wp-srv/sports/longterm/general/povich/launch/gehrig39.htm.

3. Rick Dempsey, interviewed by the author, October 30, 2019.

4. Dempsey, interviewed by the author, October 30, 2019.

5. Sara Kaden, "Nobody Doesn't Like Louie G," *MoreGehrig: Extensive Gehrig Info Source*, 2002, accessed April 9, 2019, http://moregehrig.tripod.com/id15.html.

6. Ray Robinson, *Iron Horse: Lou Gehrig in His Time* (New York: W. W. Norton, 1990), 181.

7. Frank Graham, *Lou Gehrig: A Quiet Hero* (Eau Claire, WI: E. M. Hale, 1942), 145.

8. Harry Grayson, "McCarthy Recalls Pine St. Baseball Parade That Turned Him from Cricket to Diamond," quoted in John McMurray, "Joe McCarthy," Society for American Baseball Research, last revised February 17, 2021, https://sabr.org/bioproj/person/joe-mccarthy/.

9. Grayson quoted in McMurray, "Joe McCarthy," accessed April 10, 2019.

10. "McCarthy Admits Yankees' Hurling Must Stiffen Much," *Philadelphia Record*, February 23, 1931, quoted in McMurray.

11. Robinson, *Iron Horse*, 152–53.

12. Povich, "'Iron Horse' Breaks."

13. Mike Buddie, interviewed by the author, November 15, 2019.

14. Jonathan Eig, *Luckiest Man: The Life and Death of Lou Gehrig* (New York: Simon & Schuster, 2005), 147.

CHAPTER 9

1. Eleanor Gehrig and Joseph Durso, *My Luke and I* (New York: Thomas Y. Crowell, 1976), 153.

2. Joseph Wancho, "Bill Dickey," Society for American Baseball Research, accessed April 12, 2019, https://sabr.org/bioproj/person/bill-dickey/.

3. Thomas Rogers, "Bill Dickey, the Yankee Catcher and Hall of Famer, Dies at 86." *New York Times*, November 13, 1993, https://www.nytimes.com/1993/11/13/obituaries/bill-dickey-the-yankee-catcher-and-hall-of-famer-dies-at-86.html.

4. Bill Dickey, interview by Rod Roberts, April 27, 1987, accession number BL-7285-94-1, call number CTA 20, National Baseball Hall of Fame and Museum, Cooperstown, NY.

5. Wancho, "Bill Dickey."

6. "Bill Dickey," National Baseball Hall of Fame and Museum, accessed April 15, 2019, https://baseballhall.org/hall-of-famers/dickey-bill.

7. Dickey, interview by Roberts, April 27, 1987.

8. "Bill Dickey," National Baseball Hall of Fame and Museum.

9. Rogers, "Bill Dickey, the Yankee Catcher."

10. Rogers.

11. Wancho, "Bill Dickey."

12. Dickey, interview by Roberts, April 27, 1987.

13. Dickey, interview by Roberts.

14. Dickey, interview by Roberts.

CHAPTER 10

1. "Galloping down Memory Lane," *Sporting News*, April 22, 1937.

2. Andy McGaffigan, interviewed by the author, October 10, 2019.

3. James Lincoln Ray, "Lou Gehrig," Society for American Baseball Research, accessed April 26, 2019, https://sabr.org/bioproj/person/lou-gehrig/.

4. Frank Graham, *Lou Gehrig: A Quiet Hero* (Eau Claire, WI: E. M. Hale, 1942), 222.

CHAPTER 11

1. Dom Amore, "Speech Class: 75 Years Ago, a Dignified Lou Gehrig Bows Out," *Morning Call*, July 7, 2014, accessed May 1, 2019, https://www.mcall.com/sports/mc-xpm-2014-07-07-mc-lou-gehrig-speech-anniversary-yankees-0707-20140707-story.html.

2. "Letter from Grantland Rice to Eleanor Gehrig, 1949 March 30," National Baseball Hall of Fame and Museum digital collection, accessed May 1, 2019, https://collection.baseballhall.org/PASTIME/letter-grantland-rice-eleanor-gehrig-1949-march-30-1#page/1/mode/1up.

3. John Kieran, "The Sports of the Times," *New York Times*, August 13, 1933, S2, quoted in Erik Randall, "Lou Gehrig: Hero and Icon in Turbulent Times,"

History for Free: A History Blog Specializing in American History, June 24, 2013, https://historyforfree.com/2013/06/24/lou-gehrig-hero-and-icon-in-turbulent-times/.

4. Gil Patterson, interviewed by the author, November 4, 2019.

5. Greg Cadaret, interviewed by the author, November 9, 2019.

6. Tony Castro, *Gehrig & the Babe: The Friendship and the Feud* (Chicago: Triumph Books, 2018), 206.

7. Leonard Shapiro, "Getcher Red-Hot Memorabilia Right Here!," *Washington Post*, May 11, 1996, https://www.washingtonpost.com/archive/lifestyle/1996/05/11/getcher-red-hot-memorabilia-right-here/efebfd5a-9062-4833-b326-5e3a449823f1/.

8. Cadaret, interviewed by the author, November 9, 2019.

CHAPTER 12

1. Mike Buddie, interviewed by the author, November 15, 2019.

2. Eleanor Gehrig and Joseph Durso, *My Luke and I* (New York: Thomas Y. Crowell, 1976), 228.

3. Tara Krieger, "Eleanor Gehrig," Society for American Baseball Research, accessed June 4, 2019, https://sabr.org/bioproj/person/eleanor-gehrig/.

CHAPTER 13

1. Eleanor Gehrig and Joseph Durso, *My Luke and I* (New York: Thomas Y Crowell, 1976), 35–36.

2. "Anna Christina *Facke (Flack)* Gehrig," Find a Grave, accessed December 3, 2019, https://www.findagrave.com/memorial/65284294/christina-gehrig.

3. Kevin Viola, *Lou Gehrig*, 2nd ed. (Minneapolis: Lerner Publishing Group, 2012), 8.

4. Paul Warburton, *Signature Seasons: Fifteen Baseball Legends at Their Most Memorable, 1908–1949* (Jefferson, NC: McFarland, 2010), 132.

CHAPTER 14

1. Frank Graham, *Lou Gehrig: A Quiet Hero* (Eau Claire, WI: E. M. Hale, 1942), 159.

2. Graham, *Lou Gehrig*, 159.

3. Eleanor Gehrig and Joseph Durso, *My Luke and I* (New York: Thomas Y Crowell, 1976), 136.

4. Gehrig and Durso, *My Luke and I*, 33.

5. Gehrig and Durso, 55.

6. Gehrig and Durso, 108.
7. Fred Kipp, interviewed by the author, November 19, 2019.

CHAPTER 15

1. Jonathan Eig, *Luckiest Man: The Life and Death of Lou Gehrig* (New York: Simon and Schuster, 2005), 328.
2. Mike Buddie, interviewed by the author, November 15, 2019.
3. Richard Sandomir, "The Good Boy of Baseball: The Final Days of Lou Gehrig," accessed August 7, 2019, Bronx Zoo, https://bxzoo.com/viewtopic.php?t=1413.
4. Rick Dempsey, interviewed by the author, October 30, 2019.

EPILOGUE

1. Shirley Povich, "This Morning with Shirley Povich: Iron Horse Breaks as Athletic Greats Meet in His Honor," *Washington Post*, July 4, 1939.
2. Povich, "Iron Horse Breaks."
3. Gil Patterson, interviewed by the author, November 4, 2019.
4. Grantland Rice, *The Tumult and the Shouting: My Life in Sport* (New York: A. S. Barnes, 1954), 149.
5. "Sick Boy Promised Ruth Homer Dies at 74," *Los Angeles Times*, January 11, 1990, https://www.latimes.com/archives/la-xpm-1990-01-11-sp-572-story.html.
6. Dave Anderson and Bill Pennington, eds., *The New York Times Story of the Yankees, 1903–Present: 390 Articles, Profiles & Essays* (New York: Black Dog & Leventhal Publishers, 2012), 111.
7. Jonathan Eig, *Luckiest Man: The Life and Death of Lou Gehrig* (New York: Simon and Schuster, 2005), 315.
8. "Looking Back at Lou Gehrig Appreciation Day," JUGS Sports blog, August 28, 2018, https://jugssports.com/looking-back-at-lou-gehrig-appreciation-day/.
9. Mike Buddie, interviewed by the author, November 15, 2019.
10. "Memorials and Tributes to Gehrig," *MoreGehrig: Extensive Gehrig Info Source*, accessed August 12, 2020, http://moregehrig.tripod.com/id41.html.
11. Vinnie Anella, interviewed by the author, August 14, 2020.
12. Anella, interviewed by the author, August 14, 2020.
13. "Letter from James Farley to Lou Gehrig, 1939 July 05," National Baseball Hall of Fame digital collection, accessed August 26, 2020, https://collection.baseballhall.org/PASTIME/letter-james-farley-lou-gehrig-1939-july-05-1#page/1/mode/1up.

AFTERWORD

1. "Gehrig, 'Iron Man' of Baseball, Dies at the Age of 37," *New York Times*, June 3, 1941.
2. Greg Cadaret, interviewed by the author, November 9, 2019.
3. Steve Wulf, "An Awful Lot to Live For," *ESPN*, July 3, 2014, https://www.espn.com/mlb/story/_/id/11159148/mlb-remembering-lou-gehrig-farewell-speech.
4. Bill Francis, "The Wright Stuff," National Baseball Hall of Fame and Museum, accessed August 12, 2019, https://baseballhall.org/discover-more/stories/short-stops/the-wright-stuff.
5. William C. Kashatus, *Lou Gehrig: A Biography* (Westport, CT: Greenwood Press, 2004).
6. Kashatus, *Lou Gehrig*, 112–13.
7. Kashatus, 112–13.
8. Harvey Frommer, *Five O'Clock Lightning: Babe Ruth, Lou Gehrig, and the Greatest Baseball Team in History, the 1927 New York Yankees* (Hoboken, NJ: John Wiley & Sons, 2008), 198.

APPENDIX

1. "Gehrig Delivers His Famous Speech at Yankee Stadium," filmed July 4, 1939, video, 1:09, https://www.youtube.com/watch?v=nNLKPaThYkE.
2. Compiled from multiple news sources on March 31, 2022.
3. Shirley Povich, "This Morning with Shirley Povich: 'Iron Horse' Breaks as Athletic Greats Meet in His Honor," *Washington Post*, July 4, 1939.
4. Edward T. Murphy, "History of Baseball: Iron Man Is Moved to Tears," *New York Sun*, July 5, 1939, 29.
5. "Gehrig Delivers His Famous Speech."
6. Rosaleen Doherty, "Lou Gehrig Retires, Gives 'Luckiest Man on the Face of the Earth' Speech at Yankee Stadium in 1939," *New York Daily News*, July 3, 2015, https://www.nydailynews.com/services/new-york-then-now/bronx/sports-rewind-lou-gehrig-retires-luckiest-man-article-1.2041915.
7. Doherty, "Lou Gehrig Retires."
8. Doherty.
9. Doherty.
10. Sid Feder, "Lou Gehrig Sobs as 62,000 Pay Tribute," *San Diego Union*, July 4, 1939 (sourced from the Associated Press); Doherty.
11. Rud Rennie, "Ailing First Baseman, Sobbing after Honors by La Guardia and Farley, Thrills Stadium Throng as He Calls Himself Luckiest Man on Earth," *New York Herald Tribune*, July 5, 1939.
12. Doherty, "Lou Gehrig Retires"; Povich, "'Iron Horse' Breaks."

13. Stanley Frank, "Tribute Paid to Iron Horse Has No Equal in Baseball," *New York Post*, July 5, 1939.

14. Doherty, "Lou Gehrig Retires."

15. Feder, "Lou Gehrig Sobs"; Doherty.

16. Doherty.

17. Stanley Frank, "Tribute Paid"; Doherty.

18. "Gehrig Delivers His Famous Speech."

19. "Gehrig Delivers His Famous Speech at Yankee Stadium," filmed July 4, 1939, video, 1:09, https://www.youtube.com/watch?v=nNLKPaThYkE.

20. Sara Kaden, "ALS, the 'Other Tyrant' in Gehrig's Life," *MoreGehrig: Extensive Gehrig Info Source*, 2002, accessed June 16, 2022, https://moregehrig.tripod.com/id3.html.

SELECTED BIBLIOGRAPHY

References have been chosen that contributed important statistical data, relevant quotations, or other information that helped to accurately depict Gehrig's life and speech. As of March 22, 2022, the Baseball Reference website (baseball-reference.com) listed statistical information, available elsewhere from numerous sources, for each player discussed in this book. The Society for American Baseball Research (sabr.org) provided background information for several players discussed in this book.

Eig, Jonathan. *Luckiest Man: The Life and Death of Lou Gehrig.* New York: Simon & Schuster, 2005.

Frommer, Harvey. *Five O'Clock Lightning: Babe Ruth, Lou Gehrig, and the Greatest Baseball Team in History, the 1927 New York Yankees.* Hoboken, NJ: John Wiley & Sons, 2008.

Gehrig, Eleanor, and Joseph Durso. *My Luke and I.* New York: Thomas Y. Cromwell, 1976.

Graham, Frank. *Lou Gehrig: A Quiet Hero.* Eau Claire, WI: E. M. Hale, 1942.

Levitt, Daniel R. *Ed Barrow: The Bulldog Who Built the Yankees' First Dynasty.* Lincoln: University of Nebraska Press, 2008.

Reichler, Joseph L., ed. *The Baseball Encyclopedia: The Complete and Official Record of Major League Baseball.* 7th ed. New York: Macmillan, 1988.

Robinson, Ray. *Iron Horse: Lou Gehrig in His Time.* New York: W. W. Norton, 1990.

Steinberg, Steve, and Lyle Spatz. *The Colonel and Hug: The Partnership That Transformed the New York Yankees.* Lincoln: University of Nebraska Press, 2015.

Wagner, Steven K. *The Four Home Runs Club: Sluggers Who Achieved Baseball's Rarest Feat.* Lanham, MD: Rowman & Littlefield, 2018.

INDEX

Aaron, Hank, 10
Afra the dog, 10, 39
Alexander, Grover Cleveland, 80
Allen, Dick, 14
Allen, Mel, 17, 154
ALS Association, 155
American League, 6, 8–9, 14–15, 20–21, 29, 31, 38, 41, 53, 66, 73, 77, 83–84, 88, 131, 151, 161
    first Yankee pennant in, 51
    Gehrig MVP award for, 126
    president Ban Johnson of, 72
    president Will Harridge of, 160
    RBI record for, 11
Amyotrophic lateral sclerosis (ALS), 25–26, 30, 155, 158–59
    Gehrig and, 5, 10, 21, 27–28, 31, 36, 39, 62, 81, 86, 91, 97, 105–6, 127, 137, 139, 143, 157, 162
Anella, Vinnie, 155
Appel, Marty, 1
Arkansas Travelers, 87
Armour, Mark, 63
Associated Press, xiv, xvi, xvii
Atlantic League, 61
Austin, Gene, 132

Baker Field, 120
Baltimore Orioles, 13, 149–50
Banks, Ernie, 10

Barrow, Ed, 29, 54, 63, 79–80, 105, 147, 150, 153
    birth of, 60
    death of, 11, 144, 160
    diagnosis released by, 86
    farewell speech and, xvi, 1, 10, 57–58, 64, 111, 113, 144
    Gehrig locker retired by, 62
    Gehrig number retired by, 59
    Gehrig signed by, 37, 49, 57
    gun ownership supported by, 59
    heart attack suffered by, 160
    Lou Gehrig Appreciation Day and, 5, 62
    managerial experience of, 61
    as manager of Red Sox by, 61
    minor-league service of, 61
    parents of, 60
    perpetuation of Gehrig streak and, 60
    retirement of, 62, 160
    Ruth converted to hitter by, 61, 151
    as Yankees president, 111
    Yankees success and, 62
Barrow, Effie, 60 [mother of EB]
Barrow, John, 60 [father of EB]
Baseball Magazine, 105
Baseball Research Journal, 105
Baseball Writers Association of America, 4

Bench, Johnny, 13
Bendix, William, 161
Bengough, Benny, 42, 44
Berra, Yogi, 89, 162
Bonds, Barry, 10
Book-Cadillac Hotel, 76
Boston Red Sox, 18, 21, 42, 44, 47, 61, 80, 88–89, 150, 155, 161
Boutilier, Brother Matthias, 150
Brett, George, 13
Briggs Stadium, 21, 27
Brooklyn Dodgers, 18, 44, 63, 72
Brown, Warren, 104
Brunsvold, Sara K., 24
Buddie, Mike, 81, 116, 143, 153
Buffalo Bisons, 79

Cadaret, Greg, 107, 111, 158
Century of Progress, 134
Chapman, Ben, 27, 80
Charcot, Jean Martin, 26
Charcot's disease, 26
Chicago Cubs, 44, 77, 80, 129, 151, 160–61
Chicago Herald-Examiner, 105
Chicago Saint Xavier Academy High School, 132
Chicago White Sox, 18, 87, 89, 133
Christ Episcopal Church, 86, 154, 157
Cincinnati Reds, 13, 22, 71–72, 111
Clarke, Fred, 61
Cleveland Indians, 84
Coakley, Andy, 49–50
Cobb, Ty, 69
Colbert, Claudette, 35
Columbia Grammar School, 49
Columbia University, 3, 18, 49–50, 65, 120–21, 130, 137, 159
  Gehrig enrolls at, 8, 93
  Gehrig faces expulsion from, 36
  Gehrig suspended by, 95, 124
  scholarship fund at, 154

Chicago World's Fair, 9, 116, 132, 134
Combs, Earle, 27, 42, 78, 109
Comiskey Park, 18, 130, 133, 135
Cooper, Gary, 24, 86, 158
Crosetti, Frank, 45–46, 161
Crosley Field, 13
Cubs Park, 16

Dahlgren, Babe, 3, 40, 46, 111
Daniels, Christine, 42
Dempsey, Rick, 40, 76, 78, 144, 161
Detroit Tigers, 21, 27, 61, 69
Devery, William, 51
Dickey, Bill, xvi, 1, 4, 27, 35, 45–46, 59, 78, 83, 92, 102, 104–5, 138, 144, 157
  birth of, 87
  death of, 89
  early years of, 87
  farewell speech and, 10, 65, 147
  Gehrig ALS and, 85
  Gehrig ALS battle and, 162
  Gehrig beaning and, 84
  Gehrig death and, 11
  at Gehrig memorial service, 87
  Gehrig rooms with, 84
  in Hall of Fame, 89, 162
  in *The Pride of the Yankees*, 86
  Lou Gehrig Appreciation Day and, 90
  minor-league service of, 87
  WWII bonds purchased by, 87
  WWII service of, 88
Dickey, George "Skeeter" [brother of BD], 89
Dieges & Clust Jewelers, 4
DiMaggio, Joe, 10, 23, 33, 46, 61, 143, 161
Dodger Stadium, 14
Doherty, Rosaleen, xiv, xvi, xvii, 5
Donovan, "Wild" Bill, 72
Douglas, Stephen, 148

Dugan, Joe, 42, 44, 123
Dunn, Jack, 150

Eastern League, 8, 61, 95
Eig, Jonathan, 82
Eleanor and Lou Gehrig MDA/ALS Multidisciplinary Care Center, 159
ESPN, 151

Farley, James A., 5, 76, 107–8, 152, 156
Farrell, Frank, 51
Feller, Bob, 89, 161
Fenway Park, 18
Fisher, Fred, 134
Fitzgerald, John F. "Honey Fitz," 160
Five O'clock Lightning [Frommer], 19
Flaherty, Patsy, 79
Fleischmann Mountain Tourists, 71
Fletcher, Art, 27, 134
Ford, Whitey, 16
Foster, John, 105
Foxx, Jimmie, 21
Franklin Millionaires, 79
Fred, Dr. Herbert L., 23
Frick, Ford, 160
Frommer, Harvey, 19

Garvey, Steve, 13
Gehrig, Anna Christina [sister of LG], 123
Gehrig, Anna Christina F. [mother of LG], 6, 105, 116, 120–21, 126, 139, 152
  birth of, 122
  culinary talents of, 123
  death of children and, 123
  dying Gehrig visited by, 127
  Eleanor sued by, 158
  farewell speech and, 147
  Gehrig wedding and, 135

marriage of, 113
popularity of, 159
rift with Ruth and, 125
streak prolonged by, 124
thyroid surgery of, 125
Gehrig, Eleanor [wife of LG], 5, 10, 39, 54–55, 62, 84, 86, 102, 106, 121, 126, 130, 133, 135–36, 138, 141–42, 148, 153, 162
  ALS center established by, 159
  ambulance donated by, 154
  birth of, 131
  death of, 159
  early years of, 114–15, 132
  farewell speech and, 113, 35, 147
  Gehrig funeral attended by, 158
  Lou Gehrig Appreciation Day and, 99
  Lou Gehrig death and, 116, 127, 129, 144
  Lou Gehrig funeral and, 117
  Lou Gehrig Memorial Fund and, 104
  marriage of, 125, 129
  Mayo Clinic consultation with, 31
  songwriting by, 134
  suit against, 158
  The Pride of the Yankees and, 158
Gehrig, Heinrich [father of LG], 6, 57, 117, 120–21, 123–24, 139, 160
  birth of, 122
  farewell speech and, 113, 147
  Gehrig death and, 127
  genealogy of, 122
  immigration by, 122
  popularity of, 159
Gehrig, Johann Philipp [grandfather of LG], 122
Gehrig, Lou, 2–4, 12–15, 19, 25–30, 32, 35, 37, 40, 42–43, 45–48, 50, 52–53, 55–57, 60–61, 64, 66–67,

Gehrig, Lou *(continued)*
    69–70, 74–75, 77, 80, 82–83,
    88–89, 91–92, 94–96, 98–101,
    103, 108, 110, 112, 115, 117–24,
    126, 128, 130, 132–33, 136,
    139–40, 142, 145–46, 148, 153
  All-Century Team represented by,
    24
  AL All-Star team represented by, 21
  ALS and, 5, 21, 62, 86, 106, 127,
    137, 143, 157–58, 162
  ALS center and, 159
  beaning of, 84
  birth of, 6, 23
  college enrollment by, 93
  Commerce High and, 18
  Commerce High graduation by, 8
  death of, 11, 23, 81, 86–87, 116,
    127, 143–44, 154–55, 157
  farewell speech by, xiii–xviii, 10, 17,
    34, 38, 49, 58, 68, 73, 81, 109,
    113–14, 144, 147, 155–56, 158,
    160
  four home-runs game by, 9, 20, 97
  fund in memory of, 104, 152
  funeral for, 81, 86, 154, 157
  Giants tryout by, 7, 36
  Habein letter about, 39
  Inter-City Baseball Championship
    and, 16, 93
  locker retired for, 63
  Lou Gehrig Appreciation Day and,
    17, 31, 33, 41, 59, 62, 65, 76,
    78, 81, 87, 90, 97, 102, 105, 107,
    109, 152, 157
  marriage of, 116, 125, 129, 131,
    134, 138
  Mayo Clinic treatment of, 31, 85
  memorial service for, 87
  New York State Baseball
    Championship and, 7
  number retired for, 59, 62
  Parole Board appointment for, 22,
    141
  postage stamp of, 154
  in *Rawhide*, 10, 54, 59
  retirement of, 16, 22, 111
  scholarship fund memorializing, 154
  The Pride of the Yankees and, 86,
    158
  wedding of, 125, 135
Gehrig, Sophie Louise [sister of LG],
  123
Gillick, Pat, 64
Goldman, Steven, 11
Goldwyn, Samuel, 158
Gomez, Lefty, 45–46
Grabiner, Dorothy, 135
Graham, Frank, 68, 70, 78, 98
Greenberger, Robert, 21
Griffith Stadium, 15, 18
Guerrero, Pedro, 14

Habein, Harold C., 39
Hammond Times, 129
Harding, President Warren G., 20
Harridge, Will, 160
Harris, Bucky, 102
Harry M. Stevens Co., 4
Hartford Courant, 103
Hartford Senators, 8, 95
Hawking, Stephen, 25–26
Henrich, Tommy, 46, 155
High School of Commerce, 7, 15, 18
Hitler, Adolph, 87
Hoyt, Waite, 42, 44, 48, 109
Huggins, James [father of MH], 71
Huggins, Miller, 19, 51, 54, 61–62, 66,
  69, 79, 88, 147
  birth of, 71
  death of, 70, 73, 105, 134
  farewell speech and, xvi, 1, 10, 65,
    68, 73, 113
  first pennant won by, 72

first MLB championship won by, 96
Gehrig meets, 68
minor-league service of, 71
Pipp replacd by, 67
as player manager, 72
Yankees hiring of, 47
Huggins, Sarah [mother of MH], 71
Hunter, Jim "Catfish," 26
Huston, Tillinghast L'Hommedieu "Cap," 47, 51, 72
Hyde Park High School, 132

Indianapolis Indians, 79
International League, 61
Interstate League, 71
Iron Horse [Robinson], 60, 80
Irwin, Arthur, 93, 95

Jackson, Reggie, 47
Jacob Ruppert Brewery, 49
Johnny Welaj Appreciation Day, 17
Johnson, Ban, 72
Jordan, Michael, 151

Kahn, James M., 27–28
Kensico Cemetery, 154, 157, 159
Kennedy, President John F., 160
Kieran, Alma [first wife of JK], 106
Kieran, John, 35–36, 102, 104
  poem by, 4, 90–91, 105–6, 139
Kieran, Margaret [second wife of JK], 139
King, Martin Luther, 6
Kipp, Fred, 38, 134
Koenig, Mark, 42, 44
Krichell, Paul, 57
  Gehrig introduced to Barrow by, 49
  Gehrig scouted by, 37
Krieger, Tara, 116
Kuhn, Bowie, 14

La Guardia, Fiorello, 5, 22–23, 76, 107, 139–42, 152, 154
Landis, Kenesaw Mountain, 52, 96, 160
Lane Technical High School, 16
Lardner, Ring, 106
Lazzeri, Tony, 24, 42, 44, 78, 88, 109, 123
Lead Belly, 25
Levitt, Dan, 63
Lieb, Fred, 102, 104–6, 135–36
Lieb, Mary [wife of FL], 105
Lincoln, Abraham, 6, 148
Los Angeles Dodgers, 13–14
Los Angeles Times, 9, 42
Lou Gehrig Appreciation Day, 17, 31, 33, 41, 59, 62, 65, 78, 87, 102, 107–9, 157
Lou Gehrig Field, 159
Lou Gehrig Memorial Fund, 104, 154
Louisville Colonels, 79

Mack, Connie, 21, 44, 162
Mansfield Haymakers, 71
Mantle, Mickey, 10, 16, 22, 33–34, 81
Maris, Roger, 16, 161
Mayo, Charles, 31
Mayo Clinic, 5, 22, 31, 39, 63, 86, 106, 139
McCarthy, Elizabeth "Babe" [wife of JM], 29, 80
McCarthy, Joe, xvi, 28–29, 35, 59, 61–62, 78, 89, 105, 111, 113, 138, 157
  birth of, 79
  death of, 80, 161
  end of Gehrig streak and, 30, 86
  farewell speech and, xvi, 1, 65, 75–77, 82, 147
  Gehrig death and, 11, 81
  Gehrig streak preserved by, 81
  Hall of Fame and, 80

McCarthy, Joe *(continued)*
  Lou Gehrig Appreciation Day and,
    5, 10, 75, 81, 107, 114, 152
  as Louisville manager, 79
  marriage of, 80
  minor-league venues of, 79
  resignation of, 88
  retirement of, 162
  Ruppert funeral and, 160
McGaffigan, Andy, 30, 33, 35, 38, 94
McGraw, John, 36, 93–94, 96, 98–99
  retirement of, 20, 97
  successor to, 95
Mercer, Sid, 5, 76, 106–9
Meusel, Bob, 19, 42–43, 48, 78, 88
Meusel, Emil "Irish" [brother of BM], 43
Meyer, Buddy, 80
Meyer, Oscar, 132
Milan, Clyde, 69
Milford Little League, 159
Mills, Wilbur, 87
Monday, Rick, 14
Moore, Wilcy, 42
Mount Olivet Cemetery, 80, 161
Murray, Jim, 9

National Baseball Hall of Fame, 78, 82, 89, 93, 151, 160–62
  Gehrig's induction to, 23, 40
  Gehrig trophy displayed at, 106
  version of Gehrig speech by, xiii
  Veterans Committee for, 44, 80, 161
National League, 49, 77, 92
  McCarthy's first MLB pennant in, 80
  president Ford Frick of, 160
Nee, Johnny, 88
New York American, 106, 109
New York City Parole Board, 22, 86, 191, 142
  Gehrig appointed to, 141

New York Daily News, xiv, xvi, xvii, xviii, 5
New York Giants, xvi, 1, 4, 7, 10, 18, 20, 36, 43–44, 91–96, 98–99, 137
New York Highlanders, 7, 51
New York National Guard, 50
New York-Presbyterian Hospital/Columbia University, 159
New York Sun, xiv, xv, 27, 80, 105–6
New York Times, xiv, 4, 62, 67, 86, 102, 105–6, 139
New York Tribune, 106
New York Yankees, xiii, 2–5, 7–11, 15–16, 18–19, 21–24, 27, 29–30, 34–35, 37–38, 40, 42–45, 47–48, 51–54, 57, 59, 62–63, 65–68, 70, 72–73, 75, 77–78, 80–84, 86–94, 96–97, 101–7, 109–11, 113–14, 124–27, 130–35, 138, 140, 143–44, 147–162
  farewell speech and, 58
  Habein letter released by, 39
  Lou Gehrig Appreciation Day and, 31, 41
  Mickey Mantle Day and, 33
  Ruth purchased by, 61
  signing of Gehrig by, 49, 95
Niagara University, 79
Niven, David, 26
Noren, Irv, 6, 10

Oakland Athletics, 67
O'Dwyer, William O., 161
Old Timers Association of Denver, 4
O'Leary, Paul, 63
Ott, Mel, 10
Otto, Walter C.G., 84

Pacific Coast League, 42
Painter, Earle V. "Doc," 5
Patterson, Gil, 67, 105, 148
Pennock, Herb, 42, 44, 109–11

Perry, Kitty, 129, 135
Pfeiffer, Sophia Johanna [grandmother of LG], 122
Phi Delta Theta, 8
Philadelphia Athletics, 9, 15, 20–21, 43–45, 80, 97, 110, 161
Philadelphia News, 105
Philadelphia Phillies, 14, 64
Pipgras, George, 42
Pipp, Wally, 38, 42, 44, 67–68
Pittsburgh Pirates, 42
Polo Grounds, 18, 93, 95, 98
Povich, Shirley, xv, 17, 39, 147
Power, Tyrone, 114
Public School 132, 7

Rawhide, 10, 54, 59
Ray, James Lincoln, 20
Rebecca of Sunnybrook Farm, 158
Repoz, Roger, 16, 22
Rice, Grantland, 22, 102–6, 151
Rickey, Branch, 63–64
Ripken Jr., Cal, 13, 155
Roberts, Morganna, 13
Robinson, Bill "Bojangles," 86, 158, 161
Robinson, Jackie, 63, 155
Robinson, Ray, 60, 78, 80–81
Robinson, Wilbert, 72
Rolfe, Red, 46
Roosevelt, President Franklin Delano, 6
Root, Charlie, 151
Roscoe, Mike, 2
Rose, Pete, 13
Ruffing, Red, 45–46
Runyon, Damon, 106
Ruppert Jr., Jacob, xvi, 1, 47, 52–55, 59, 65, 105, 111, 113, 147, 159, 161
 birth of, 49
 brewery inherited by, 51
 as congressman, 51
 co-owner bought out by, 72
 death of, 49, 61, 160
 farewell speech and, 10, 11, 160
 funeral for, 70, 86, 160
 McCarthy hired by, 80
 rank conferred upon, 50
 Yankees purchased by, 66
 Yankee Stadium built by, 48
Rutgers College, 37, 49
Ruth, Babe, xiii, 10, 15, 17, 19–21, 23–24, 42, 48–49, 53, 65, 67–68, 70, 73, 88, 94, 98, 115, 121, 123, 125–26, 134, 137, 139, 145, 149, 153, 156, 162
 birth of, 148
 Bustin' Babes with, 138
 called shot by, 151
 with cancer, 161
 death of, 44, 155, 160–61
 farewell speech by, 147
 funeral for, 161
 Gehrig death and, 11, 144
 Hall of Fame joined by, 151
 as home run leader, 9, 107
 Lou Gehrig Appreciation Day and, 5–6, 41, 54, 75–76, 81, 109, 152
 Monument Park and, 81
 as MVP, 151
 Red Sox purchase of, 47, 61
 retirement of, 111
 Ruppert funeral and, 160
 Ruth homers for sick boy during, 151
 St. Mary's Industrial School and, 150
Ruth, Claire [second wife of BR], 109, 125, 144
Ruth, Dorothy [daughter of BR], 125
Ruth, George, Sr. [father of BR], 148
Ruth, Helen [first wife of BR], 125
Ruth, Kate [mother of BR], 148

Ruth, Mamie [sister of BR], 149
Ryan, Nolan, 13

St. Louis Browns, 49, 84
St. Louis Cardinals, 53, 63, 66, 72, 101, 151
St. Mary's Industrial School for Boys, 150
St. Patrick's Cathedral, 160–61
St. Paul Saints, 71
Saks Fifth Avenue, 116, 133–34
Salt Lake City Bees, 42
Sax, Steve, 14
Schang, Wally, 42, 44
Schilling, Curt, 154
Schilling, Gehrig [son of CS], 154
Scott, Everett, 42, 44
Searcy High School, 87
Selkirk, George, 46
Selznick, David O., 35
Sewell, Joe, 84
Shantz, Bobby, 15, 24
Shawkey, Bob, 42, 44, 45
Shibe Park, 19
Sigma Nu, 8
Smith, Al, 160
Smith, Red, 62
Society for American Baseball Research, 20, 63
Sporting News, 89, 105
Steinbrenner, George, 38
Stengel, Casey, 89
Stevens, Harry M., 110–11
Sullivan, Ed, 161
Sylvester, John Dale, 151–52

Temple, Shirley, 158
Tenor, John, 160
Terry, Bill, 77, 93, 95, 97, 99
The Babe Ruth Story, 161
The Life of Lou Gehrig: Told by a Fan [Brunsvold], 24

The Pride of the Yankees, 86, 158–59
Toledo Mud Hens, 79
Toronto Blue Jays, 64
Twitchell Jr., Frank [brother of EG], 5, 115
  death of, 114
Twitchell Sr., Frank [father of EG], 116, 131
  Chicago riots and, 133
  early life of, 114
  future wife and, 114
  Gehrig speech omission of, 113
  marital separation of, 113
  marriage of, 113
  as pricemaker, 114
Twitchell, Nellie [mother of EG]
  birth of, 131
  divorce consultation for, 114
  early life of, 114
  Eleanor lives with, 162
  farewell speech and, 10, 113, 147
  future husband of, 114
  Gehrig funeral and, 117
  meets Gehrig mother, 116

United Press International, xiv
United States Brewers Association, 50
United States Military Academy at West Point
University of Cincinnati, 71

Vila, Joe, 80, 105
Virdon, Bill, 49, 53, 57

Wagner, Honus, 61
Wagner, Robert, 160
Walnut Hills High School, 71
Wanninger, Pee Wee, 16
Washington Nationals, 28
Washington Post, xiv, xv, xvii, 17, 39, 147

Washington Senators, 2, 4, 17–18, 69, 80, 102, 136
Wattenberg, Col. Fred, 53–54
Weiss, George, 160
Welaj, Johnny, 17
Westin Book Cadillac Hotel, 76
White, Ray, 65, 84
Wilkes-Barre Barons, 79
Williams, Ted, 10
Wilmington Peaches, 79
World Series, 2, 4, 11, 16, 42, 51, 53, 61–63, 67, 77, 80, 91–93, 97–98, 101, 126, 129, 131, 136, 140, 160
  Black Sox scandal and, 133
  Gehrig's final representation in, 22, 141
  Gehrig sits out the, 96
  Ruth homers for ailing boy during, 151
Wright, Teresa, 158

Wrigley Field, 16

Yankee Stadium, xiii, 18–20, 23–24, 40, 47, 55, 57, 60, 63, 84, 88, 96, 110, 123, 125, 136, 140, 143
  Babe Ruth Day at, 161
  Ruth's final appearance at, 161
  Ruth viewing at, 155
  construction of, 48, 51
  farewell speech at, xiii, 5, 38, 39, 89, 108
  Gehrig memorial at, 87, 90
  Johnny Welaj Day at, 17
  Lou Gehrig Appreciation Day at, 10, 41, 62, 68, 75, 78, 91, 102, 107, 109, 148, 155
  Mickey Mantle Day at, 33
  Monument Park at, 81, 154
  opening of, 2, 8, 44

ABOUT THE AUTHOR

Steven K. Wagner rose from paperboy to eventually write for the legendary news service United Press International (UPI). The author of five books, Mr. Wagner is among the most prolific baseball writers over the past decade. He began his career as a staff writer and assistant bureau chief with UPI. He then joined *The Oregonian* as the Portland newspaper's Vancouver, Washington, bureau chief and later as its night crime reporter. Over the past thirty-five years, Mr. Wagner, a former editor of the Los Angeles Rams' team magazine, has freelanced extensively for the *Los Angeles Times*. His work has also appeared in the *New York Times*, *Washington Post*, *Los Angeles Times Magazine*, *Seattle Times*, *Oregon Journal*, *Oklahoma City Oklahoman*, *Portland Tribune*, *Idaho Statesman*, *Baseball America*, and many other newspapers and magazines. Mr. Wagner has been married for thirty-three years, has two grown children, and resides in Pennsylvania.

www.ingramcontent.com/pod-product-compliance
Lightning Source LLC
Chambersburg PA
CBHW070355240426
43671CB00013BA/2505